Herbert Puchta & Jeff Stranks

G. Gerngross C. H[...] [...]nes

American MORE! 2B

COMBO Student's Book

NOTE FOR TEACHERS

The pages of this Combo edition are numbered in the usual way in sequence throughout. Where the numbers are different from the original full edition Student's Book and Workbook pages, a second number is shown that looks like this: 23. This is so that the page references in full edition teacher components such as the Teacher's Resource Book can be followed easily.

HELBLING LANGUAGES

CAMBRIDGE UNIVERSITY PRESS

editora ática

editora ática

Diretora-Geral Editoras Ática e Scipione
Vera Balhestero
Gerente Editorial e de Conteúdos Didáticos
Teresa Porto
Coordenador Editorial de Línguas Estrangeiras
Luiz Tonolli
Gerente de Qualidade e Suporte
Beatriz Mendes

Assistente Editorial: Danuza Dias Gonçalves
Gerente de Revisão: Hélia de Jesus Gonsaga
Equipe de Revisão: Célia da Silva Carvalho e Gloria Cunha
Edição de Arte: Erik Taketa e Mauro Fernandes
Editoração Eletrônica: A+ Comunicação

American MORE! Combo 2B with CD-ROM/Audio CD
Hebert Puchta & Jeff Stranks
G. Gerngross, C. Holzmann, P. Lewis-Jones

Direitos desta edição cedidos à Editora Ática S.A.
Av. Otaviano Alves de Lima, 4400
Freguesia do Ó – CEP 02909-900 – São Paulo – SP
Tel.: 4003-3061
www.atica.com.br / editora@atica.com.br

Dados Internacionais de Catalogação na Publicação (CIP)
(Câmara Brasileira do Livro, SP, Brasil)

American more! : Combo : student's book / Herbert Puchta...[et al.]. -- 1. ed. -- São Paulo : Ática, 2011.
Outros autores: Jeff Stranks, Gunther Gerngross, Christian Holzmann, Peter Lewis-Jones
Obra em 8 v.
Bibliografia.

1. Inglês (Ensino fundamental) I. Puchta, Herbert. II. Stranks, Jeff. III. Gerngross, Gunther. IV. Holzmann, Christian. V. Lewis-Jones, Peter.

11-13335 CDD-372.652

Índice para catálogo sistemático:
1. Inglês : Ensino Fundamental 372.652

2012
ISBN 978 85 08 15449 4 – American MORE! Combo 2B with CD-ROM and Audio CD
ISBN 978 85 08 14804 2 – American MORE! 2 Teacher's Book

Cód. da obra CL 738261

EDITORA AFILIADA

1ª edição
2ª impressão

Impressão e acabamento: Corprint Gráfica e Editora Ltda.

Uma Publicação Abril EDUCAÇÃO

MISTO
Papel produzido a partir de fontes responsáveis
FSC® C102676

The authors would like to thank those people who have made significant contributions towards the final form of American MORE!:

Oonagh Wade and Rosamund Cantalamessa for their expertise in working on the manuscripts, their useful suggestions for improvement, and the support we got from them.

Lucia Astuti and Markus Spielmann, Helbling Languages, Ron Ragsdale and James Dingle, Cambridge University Press, for their dedication to the project and innovative publishing vision.

Our designers, Amanda Hockin, Greg Sweetnam, Quantico, Craig Cornell and Niels Gyde for their imaginative layouts and stimulating creativity. Also, our artwork assistants, Francesca Gironi and Elisa Pasqualini, for their dedicated work.

The publishers would like to thank the following illustrators: Roberto Battestini; Lucy Boden; Dan Chernett; Moreno Chiacchiera; Kelly Dyson; Michele Farella; Courtney Huddleston; Giovanni Giorgi Pierfranceschi; Pierluigi Longo; Gastone Mencherini; Giovanni Rolandi; Lorenzo Sabbatini; David Shephard; Mike Spoor; Lucilla Stellato; Patrick Welsh.

The publishers would like to thank the following for their kind permission to reproduce the following photographs and other copyright material:

Student's Book
Alamy p78, p92, p102, p119; **Can Stock Photo** p109 (Juan); **Corbis** p102 (policemen on bikes), p122 (storm chaser); **Dreamstime** p66 (tennis), p68, p69, p75 (teenage girl watching tv), p79 (native), p81 (tennis player), p82 (basketball), p85 (teenage boy with laptop), p109 (Las Vegas; Jo), p111, p119 (Brittany), p122 (tornado); **©iStockphoto.com** p66 (running; soccer; mountain biking; surfing), p69 (Greg), p72, p73, p75, p80, p81 (soccer; surfing), p82 (football), p83, p85 (ill teenage girl), p102 (Mustang; Model T Ford), p109 (canoe; Joshua Tree), p110, p112, p116, p119 (Tikal), p122 (hurricane; damage left by hurricane Katrina); **© Little, Brown** p93 (Maniac Magee); Front cover of ARTEMIS FOWL by Eoin Colfer (**Penguin Books**) p93; **Shutterstock** p64 (roller coaster), p66, p71, p75 (teenage boy running), p79, p81, p82 (baseball), p102 (Cadillac), p109 (Vancouver; Linda; Mel), p119 (roller coaster); **The Random House Group Ltd.** p93 (VickyAngel); **The Times Herald of Norristown, Penn** p92 (Jerry Spinelli).

The publishers would like to thank the following for their assistance with commissioned photographs: **Ed-Imaging** pp 64, 74, 84, 94, 104, 114; **David Tolley Ltd.** p76.

Workbook
Dreamstime p42; **©iStockphoto.com** p39 (surfing; soccer); **Shutterstock** p39; **AIP Emilio Segre Visual Archives, Lande Collection** p61.

Page numbers refer to the original version.

Every effort has been made to trace the owners of any copyright material in this book. If notified, the publisher will be pleased to rectify any errors or omissions.

	Grammar	Language Focus and Vocabulary	Skills	MORE!
UNIT 7 On the weekend	• time prepositions: *on, at, in* • present continuous for future	• sports **Sounds right** /tʃ/	• make suggestions • talk about sports • talk about future plans • read about what people do on the weekend • talk about what you do on the weekend • listen and complete diaries about people's plans for the weekend • write about your weekend **A Song 4 U** *Weekend*	Learn **MORE** through English **The feeling of happiness**
UNIT 8 It hurts!	• past continuous • superlatives	• aches and pains	• say what someone was doing • talk about sickness • read about Amazonia and answer questions • listen and complete an animal quiz • read a letter and answer questions • write a letter to a student who is ill	**Check your progress** Units 7 and 8 Learn **MORE** about culture **Sports in the United States** Read **MORE** for pleasure **The world of birds: the biggest and the smallest**
UNIT 9 Guess what?	• past continuous vs. simple past • *one/ones* • quantity *a lot of, much, many*	• emotions	• give reasons • talk about emotions • read a story and match sentences • listen to a story and order pictures • tell and listen to a story • write an ending to a story	Learn **MORE** through English **Famous modern authors for teenagers**
UNIT 10 Shouldn't we ask?	• *should/shouldn't* • conjunctions: *and/ so/but/because*	• directions and places	• use large numbers • give advice • ask for and give directions • listen and read directions • identify buildings • write an email with directions **A Song 4 U** *Looking for Liz*	**Check your progress** Units 9 and 10 Learn **MORE** about culture **The history of the car** Read **MORE** for pleasure **Looking for Keiko**
UNIT 11 It won't rain	• *will/won't* • *might/might (not)*	• weather	• make excuses • talk about the weather • read about different places and match to the correct photo • listen and draw weather symbols on a map • talk about the weather • talk about your future • write about your future	Learn **MORE** through English **Aurora Borealis—the Northern Lights**
UNIT 12 What if ...?	• *If* clauses • possessive pronouns • questions with *Whose?*	• vacations **Sounds right** /i/ /ɪ/	• talk about alternatives • suggestions and preferences • do a quiz about your book • listen and check answers to the quiz • write about your next vacation **A Song 4 U** *We are on vacation*	**Check your progress** Units 11 and 12 Learn **MORE** about culture **Extreme weather** Read **MORE** for pleasure **Strange weather stories**

UNIT 7 On the weekend

In this unit

You learn

- time prepositions: *on, at, in*
- present continuous for future
- words for sports

and then you can

- make suggestions
- talk about sports
- talk about future plans

49 **1 Listen and read.**

Harry What are you doing on Saturday, Olivia?

Olivia I think I'm going to a basketball game with Michael.

Sally Oh, we're going to Six Flags. Would you like to come along?

Olivia Six Flags? What's that?

Tony It's an amusement park. There are all kinds of different rides.

Harry ...and there's a waterslide.

Olivia I don't really like amusement parks.

Tony Why not?

Olivia Too much standing around, so maybe some other time. Besides, this Saturday I'm watching the basketball game with Michael.

Harry Alright. So what are you doing on Sunday?

Olivia I'm not sure.

Harry Well, would you like to go to a movie with me? I could pick you up from your place at seven.

Olivia Oh, now I remember. I can't. I'm having dinner at Michael's place!

2 **Match the sentence halves.**

1 Tony, Sally, and Harry
2 Six Flags is an amusement
3 Olivia doesn't want to come
4 On Saturday Olivia is
5 On Sunday Olivia can't
6 She's having dinner

a along because she doesn't like amusement parks.
b go to the movies with Harry.
c at Michael's place.
d watching a basketball game with Michael.
e are visiting Six Flags on Saturday.
f park with great rides.

Get talking Making suggestions

50 **3** **Listen and number the pictures.**

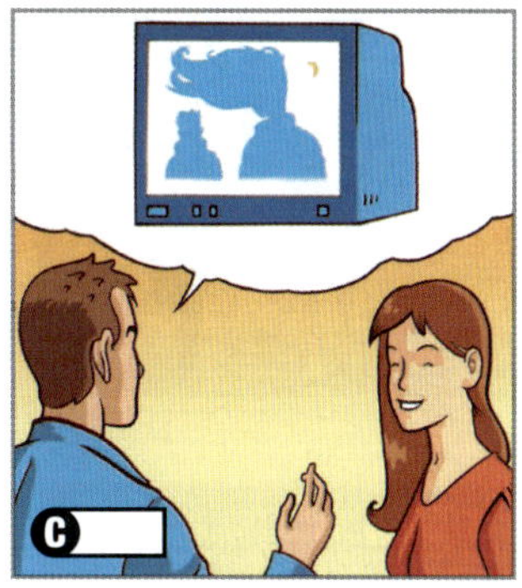

51 **4** **Listen and repeat.**

A What are we doing this weekend?
B Should we go to an amusement park?
A Yes, why not?

A What are we doing on Sunday?
B We could watch the last *Friends* season.
A I'm not too interested in that.

5 **Work with a partner. Talk about the weekend. Use the pictures and the phrases below.**

Let's…
Why don't we…?
Should we…?
We could…

go for a walk

play tennis

sleep the whole time

go to a restaurant

go to the beach

Language Focus

Vocabulary Sports

52 **1** **Write the number of the sport in the picture. Then listen and check your work.**

play:	**go:**	
1 soccer	5 mountain climbing	9 skateboarding
2 tennis	6 cycling	10 swimming
3 basketball	7 mountain biking	11 surfing
4 volleyball	8 in-line skating	12 running

Get talking Talking about sports

2 **Work with a partner. Ask and answer questions about the sports in Exercise 1.**

Do you like…?

What's your favorite… team?

Do you play / go…?

How often do you…?

Do you like watching… on TV?

Who's your favorite athlete?

Grammar

Time prepositions *on, at, in*

1 **Look at the examples and complete the rules.**

I was born **in** May.
I went to Colorado **in** 2006.
The movie starts **at** five o'clock.
On Monday we went to the library.
We went to the movies **on** May 23.

We use [1]........... with days of the week and the date.
We use [2]........... with times.
We use [3]........... with months and years.

(note, use **at** night, but **in** the morning/afternoon/evening)

2 **Fill in *on*, *at*, or *in*.**

1 .... Friday, April 17
2 .... Sunday
3 .... July
4 .... the morning
5 .... seven o'clock
6 .... Wednesday
7 .... the evening
8 .... night
9 1974

Present continuous Future

3 **Look at the dialogue on page 64 and complete the sentences with the days of the week.**

Olivia and Michael are watching a basketball game on [1]................
Sally is going to Six Flags on [2]................
Harry is going to the movies on [3]................
Olivia is having dinner with Michael on [4]................

We can use the present continuous to talk about future arrangements.

4 **Complete the sentences with the present continuous form of the verbs below. Use short forms.**

leave	come back	sell
move	~~meet~~	stay

1 John.'s meeting.. us in the city on Friday.
2 We .... to New York next year.
3 I .... home tonight.
4 They .... their house in November.
5 He .... school at the end of the year.
6 You .... from Japan on November 19.

5 **Make the following sentences negative.**

1 I'm coming to the party on Friday.
I'm not coming to the party on Friday.
2 They are arriving in Florida on Monday.
....
3 You're watching the football game on Saturday..
....
4 We're buying her a present on Monday.
....
....
5 She's doing all her homework tonight.
....
....
6 He's playing in the next volleyball match.
....
....

6 **Write questions and short answers.**

1 you / play football / this afternoon (yes) — A *Are you playing football this afternoon*? B *Yes, I am.*

2 she / make soup / for lunch (no) ....

3 they / take a vacation / in August (no) ....

4 you / play video games / tonight (yes) ....

5 he / finish his work / tomorrow (no) ....

6 we / make breakfast / tomorrow morning (yes) ....

Get talking Talking about future plans

7 **Complete the dialogue using the phrases below. Listen and check.**

53

I'm meeting   I'd love to   She didn't invite me   I'm watching

Kevin What are you doing this weekend?
Dawn Well, [1].............................. DVDs tomorrow night.
Do you want to watch them with me?
Kevin [2].............................. , but I can't.
Dawn Oh, why not?
Kevin [3].............................. Jenny. She's having a DVD party!
Dawn What? [4].............................. !

8 **Read the table and put a check (✓) next to the things you are doing. Then complete it for your partner.**

	Me	My partner
• meet friends tomorrow	☐	☐
• stay home on Sunday	☐	☐
• play volleyball tomorrow	☐	☐
• do homework on Saturday	☐	☐
• go to the gym on Saturday	☐	☐
• go to a party on the weekend	☐	☐
• do homework tonight	☐	☐
• make dinner tomorrow	☐	☐
• play football on Saturday	☐	☐

Are you meeting friends tomorrow?

No, I'm not. I'm visiting my grandparents. What about you?

Skills

Reading

1 **Read the magazine article and write the name, day, and time of day (morning, afternoon, or evening) under the pictures below.**

1 Greg, Saturday morning.

2 ....

3 ....

4 ....

5 ....

6 ....

What we do on the weekend

1 What time do you get up on weekends?

Greg On Saturdays I play soccer for the school team. The game starts at 9:00 a.m. On Sundays I stay in bed until about 10:00 a.m.

John I get up at 6 a.m. on Saturdays and Sundays because I have a paper route.

Wendy On Saturdays I get up late, about 10 a.m. On Sundays, if I go shopping I get up at 8 a.m. If I don't go, I get up about 9 a.m.

2 What do you usually do on Saturdays?

Greg Well, after lunch I sit and watch TV all afternoon. In the evening I usually hang out with my friends. We go to the movies or out to eat.

John I always do my homework on Saturday mornings. Then I know I have the rest of the weekend free. In the afternoon I go shopping with friends. In the evenings I stay home. But sometimes there's a party to go to.

Wendy In the morning I help my mom clean the house. But in the afternoon I usually go to a hockey game with my dad. We're big hockey fans, so we never miss a home game. In the evening I watch a DVD or go to a friend's house.

3 What do you usually do on Sundays?

Greg I don't do anything in the morning, but in the afternoon I go to the gym with my friends. In the evening I do my homework.

John On Sundays I go fishing with my friends. We take a packed lunch and stay all day. In the evening I just relax.

Wendy Sometimes I go to the mall. I always have to find a few hours to do my homework, usually in the afternoons. In the evenings I listen to music.

Speaking

2 **Work in pairs. Ask questions about the people in Exercise 1.**

What does Greg do on Saturday afternoons?

Where does Wendy go on Sundays?

3 **Put a check next to the activities that you do on the weekend and add two more. Then work with a partner and ask and answer questions.**

What I do on the weekend

- ☐ play sports
- ☐ get up late
- ☐ work
- ☐ go shopping
- ☐ watch sports
- ☐ watch TV
- ☐ go to the movies
- ☐ go out to eat
- ☐ go over to a friend's house
- ☐ do homework
- ☐ listen to music
- ☐ ....
- ☐ ....

Do you play a sport on the weekend?

What sport do you play?

Sounds right /tʃ/

54 **4** **Listen and repeat the chant.**

Chicken, chicken,
eggs and **ch**eese.
Some more rice?
Oh, yes, please!

Lots of **ch**icken,
lots of **ch**eese,
and some rice.
Oh, that's nice!

Listening

55 **5** **Listen to Fred and Annabel. Answer the questions.**

1 What do they want to do? 2 When do they decide to do it?

56 **6** **Listen again and complete the calendar using the words on the left.**

do homework
go shopping
go to gym
aunt arrives
go to a football game
watch TV
help Dad
Sue's party

Saturday	Sunday
morning	morning
afternoon	afternoon
evening	evening

Saturday	Sunday
morning	morning
afternoon	afternoon
evening	evening

A Song 4 U Weekend

57 **7 Read and complete the song using the words on the left. Then listen and check.**

emails
late
always
Sunday night
classes
bed

No more [1]........................ for a day or two.
It's the weekend. *(It's the weekend.)*
Stay in [2]........................ all day—got nothing to do.
It's the weekend *(It's the weekend.)*
It's the weekend. (x 6)

Get up [3]........................ then you call a friend.
On the weekend *(On the weekend.)*
The computer's on, I've got [4]........................ to send.
On the weekend *(On the weekend.)*
On the weekend. (x 6)

[5]........................ and it's already over again.
End of the weekend. *(End of the weekend.)*
Goes too quickly, it's [6]........................ the same.
End of the weekend. *(End of the weekend.)*
End of the weekend. (x 6)

Writing for your Portfolio

8 Write answers to these questions.

1 What time do you get up on the weekends?
2 What do you usually do on Saturdays?
3 What do you usually do on Sundays?

The feeling of happiness

Key words

happiness	hunt for food	produce chemicals	health
feeling	motivate	alarm	

1 **Match the pictures below with some of the key words.**

Where does HAPPINESS come from?

Happiness is the most wonderful feeling in the world. In fact, most people would like to be happy all the time. Where does happiness come from? And why is it so difficult to be happy? Read these texts and find out.

1 Thousands of years ago, life was very difficult and dangerous. There were a lot of wild animals, such as bears, mammoths, tigers, and wolves. People had to hunt these animals for food. That was dangerous, and not a lot of fun.

2 To motivate people to go hunting, the brain invented a trick: The feeling of happiness. When people hunted an animal and had something good to eat, their brain produced two chemicals, serotonin and endorphin. These chemicals make people feel happy. The brain also produced these chemicals when someone was the winner in a fight and when people spent time with friends.

3 Today, we no longer hunt such dangerous wild animals, but our brain still produces the same chemicals. For example, when we eat our favorite food, when we meet our friends, when we listen to our favorite music, when we do a good job at school, or when we play a sport and our team wins.

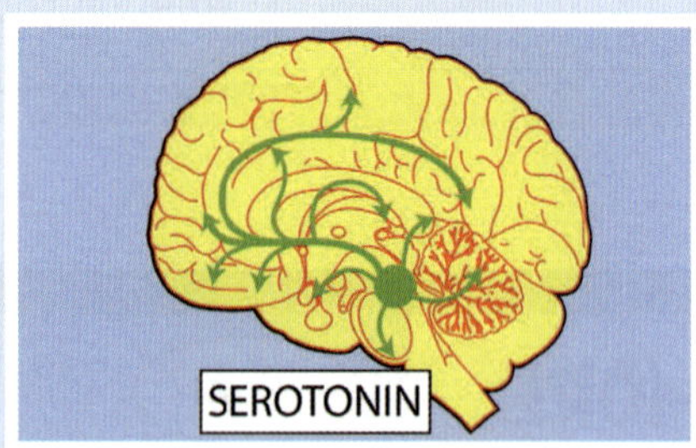

The bad news: We can't be happy all the time!

4 Let's look back thousands of years again. Imagine people sitting around a fire, eating a nice piece of tiger steak. Suddenly they hear something from behind a bush. Their brain produces another chemical, dopamine. Now the feeling is one of alarm! And their feeling of happiness was gone.

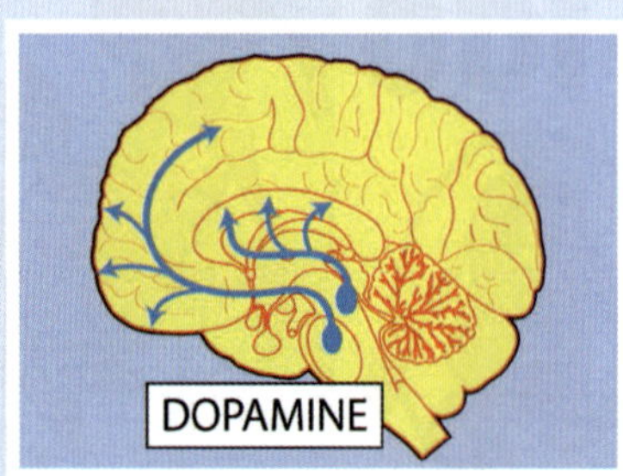

The good news: we can train our brain to be happy!

Experts say that you can train your brain to be happy. It is often small things that make us unhappy. It can help to try and think of positive things more often. Another good idea is to keep a happiness journal. Write three positive things in it every day. And before you fall asleep, think about what was good for you during the day.

Mini Project Happiness

2 **Keep a happiness journal for one week. Then make a chart of your week.**

10 = extremely happy / 0 = not happy

My happiness log **Date:** ....

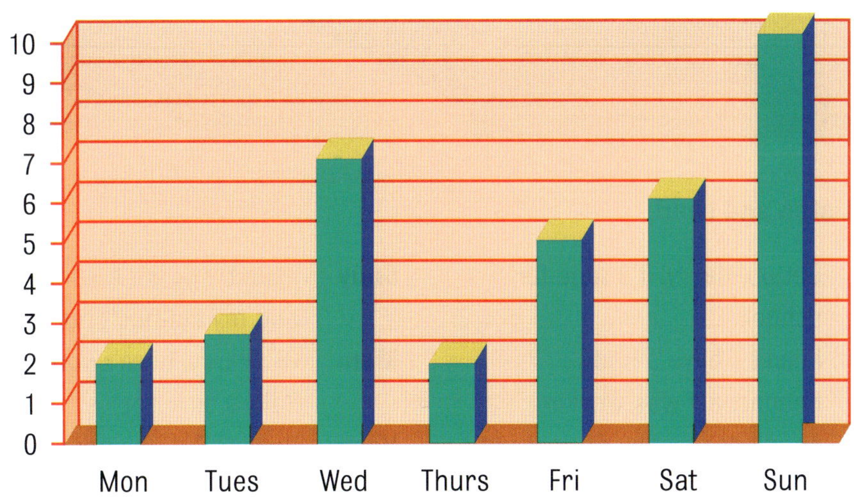

Last week was pretty good. I did something nice every day. On Monday I watched an interesting DVD about wildlife in Africa with my mom. On Tuesday my friends and I had a lot of fun at school. Thursday was not very good—I had a lot of homework! On Friday I did well in an English test. ;-) On Saturday my sister and I went to see our grandmother. We went for a walk with her dog. Sunday was great. It was my birthday!

UNIT 8 It hurts!

In this unit

You learn

- past continuous
- superlatives
- words for aches and pains

and then you can

- say what someone was doing
- talk about sickness

1 Listen and read. CD 2 – 1

Mom Get up, Harry. It's time for school.
Harry I can't. I have a bad headache. I was working on my geography project until midnight. My head hurts.
Mom Should I get you a glass of water and some aspirin?
Harry Can I have two, please? It's the worst headache in the world.
Mom Alright. Let me go and wake up Sally first.
Mom Sally! Time to get up!
Sally I can't. I've got a sore throat and my stomach hurts.
Mom OK, Harry, here's your water. Sally's sick, too.
Harry Really? But she has a math test today.
Mom How interesting! She wasn't studying very much for it yesterday. Do you have a test today, too?
Harry Yes, but it's only a science test.
Mom This is the oldest trick in the book, Harry. Get out of bed now!

2 **Complete the sentences from the dialogue.**

What Harry says:

1 My head ....
2 I was working on ....
3 It's the worst headache ....

What Sally says:

1 I've got a sore throat and ....

What Mom says:

1 Should I get you a glass .... ?
2 Sally! Time to ....
3 Get out .... !

Get talking Saying what someone was doing

2 **3** **Listen and repeat.**

A What was she doing at 7:00 p.m.?
B She was listening to music.

A What was he doing at 9:00 a.m.?
B He was taking a test.

Work with a partner. Ask and answer questions about the pictures.

A What was he doing at 10:00 a.m.?

B He was reading a book.

Language Focus

Vocabulary Aches and pains

3 **1 Match the pictures and expressions. Then listen and check.**

- ☐ stomachache
- ☐ earache
- ☐ toothache
- ☐ backache
- ☐ a headache
- ☐ a cold
- ☐ a sore throat
- ☐ my knee hurts
- ☐ dizziness
- ☐ a broken ankle

Get talking Talking about sickness

2 Work in groups of three. Act out a problem and talk about it.

3 Complete the dialogues with the words on the left. Then practice using them with a partner.

hurt
broke
toothache
head

1 A Does your .... hurt?
  B Yes, I ran into a tree.

2 A What's the matter?
  B I .... my toe during the game yesterday.

3 A Why are you walking like that?
  B I .... my ankle when I was jogging.

4 A Where are you going?
  B To the dentist. I have a ....

Grammar

Past continuous Affirmative and negative

1 **Look at the dialogue on page 74 and complete the examples.**

I [1]................... .... on my geography project until midnight.
She [2]................... .... very much for it yesterday.

We use the past continuous to talk about an action going on at a time in the past.

	Affirmative	Negative	
I/he/she/it	**was**	**wasn't**	sleep**ing** at six o'clock.
You/we/they	**were**	**weren't**	study**ing** for a test.

2 **Complete the sentences with *was / were* or *wasn't / weren't*.**

1 Jim was...... playing tennis at 10 a.m.
2 I .... speaking to my mom. It was my dad.
3 Paul and Wendy .... working.
4 She .... driving the car. I was!
5 We .... drinking lemonade. It was soda.
6 Yesterday afternoon, I .... watching a great program on TV.
7 My dad wasn't here on Saturday. He .... working at the office.

3 **Make the sentences negative.**

1 I was talking to Henry last night.
I wasn't..... talking to Henry last night.
2 We were shopping yesterday at 10:00 a.m.
....
3 They were studying in the evening.
....
4 He was having dinner at 7:00 p.m.
....
5 You were surfing the Internet this morning.
....
6 She was walking her dog last night.
....

Past continuous Questions and short answers

		Questions	Affirmative	Negative
Was	I/he/she/it	sleep**ing** at 6:00 a.m.?	Yes, I/he/she/it **was**.	No, I/he/she/it **wasn't**.
Were	you/we/they	study**ing** for a test?	Yes, you/we/they **were**.	No, you/we/they **weren't**.

4 **Write questions and short answers.**

1 you / play football / 8:00 p.m. (no)
Were you playing football at 8:00 p.m.?
No, I wasn't.
2 they / work / until 6:00 p.m. (no)
....
3 she / help / you (yes)
....
4 I / talk / to him (no)
....
5 it / rain / at 6:00 a.m. (no)
....
6 we / listen to / the teacher (yes)
....

Superlatives

5 **Look at the dialogue on page 74 and complete the examples.**

It's [1]................................... headache in the world.
This is [2]................................... trick in the book.

We use superlative adjectives to compare more than two things. The form depends on the adjective.

It's **the most** dangerous animal in the world.
His French is **the best** in the class. It's excellent.
It's **the worst** movie in the world. It's terrible.

a) If the adjective has one syllable, add [1]...................................

b) Spelling: Some adjectives double the final letter, e.g. (**hot**) *It's* ***the*** *hot**test*** *day of the year.*

If the adjective ends in *–y*, the letter *y* is replaced with [2]................., e.g. (**happy**) *It was* ***the*** *happ**iest*** *day of my life.*

c) With longer adjectives we use the words [3]................................... before the adjective.

d) The superlative of *good* is [4]...................................,
The superlative of *bad* is [5]...................................

The bumble bee bat from Thailand is the smallest mammal in the world.

6 **Write the superlative form of these adjectives.**

1 strong strongest
2 sad ....
3 lucky ....
4 hot ....
5 beautiful ....
6 boring ....
7 hungry ....
8 good ....
9 big ....
10 romantic ....
11 cold ....
12 bad ....

7 **Circle the correct word.**

1 It's *colder / coldest* than yesterday.
2 Yesterday was the *colder / coldest* day of the year.
3 She's the *more / most beautiful* actress in Hollywood.
4 I think this painting is *more / most beautiful* than the other one.
5 My bag is *heavier / heaviest* than yours.
6 What's in this bag! The *heavier / heaviest* book in the world?
7 She lives in the *bigger / biggest* house in the town.
8 My laptop is *bigger / biggest* than yours.

Skills

Reading

1 Read the text and answer the questions.

Save the rain forest!

The Amazon rain forest is one of the most important places on Earth. It produces more than 20 percent of the world's oxygen and is home to more than 2,000 medicinal plants, which help cure people who are sick. However, the rain forest is not safe. Every year people cut down many of the trees and the forest is getting smaller and smaller. About 500 years ago, more than 10 million native people lived in the Amazon rain forest. Today, there are fewer than 200,000. Native healers know all about the Amazon's important plants, but many of them are very old, and their environment is under attack. It is important for the world to know about these plants and to protect the Amazon rain forest so that native people can continue to live there.

1 Find two reasons in the text why the Amazon rain forest is important.
2 Who lives in the Amazon rain forest?
3 Why are these people important?

Listening

4 **2 Do the animal quiz, and then listen and check your answers.**

The animal quiz

1 Which is the tallest?
a ☐ a giraffe
b ☐ an ostrich
c ☐ an elephant

2 Which is the longest?
a ☐ an anaconda
b ☐ a whale shark
c ☐ a crocodile

3 Which is the fastest?
a ☐ an antelope
b ☐ a lion
c ☐ a rabbit

4 Which is the most intelligent?
a ☐ a dolphin
b ☐ a pig
c ☐ a chimpanzee

5 Which is the heaviest?
a ☐ a blue whale
b ☐ an elephant
c ☐ a rhinoceros

ANIMALS

Writing for your Portfolio

3 **Read the letter and answer the questions.**

Dear Sally,

Miss Black told us about your accident. So you were riding a horse, you fell off, and you broke your ankle! That's terrible! And now you have to stay at home for three weeks. Three weeks with no school—poor you! But don't worry, Miss Black said she's going to send you a lot of homework.

The big news is that the school football team won the game yesterday. Now we're in the finals. The game's on Saturday, so think about us.

We all miss you. Get well and come back soon!

Your friends in English class

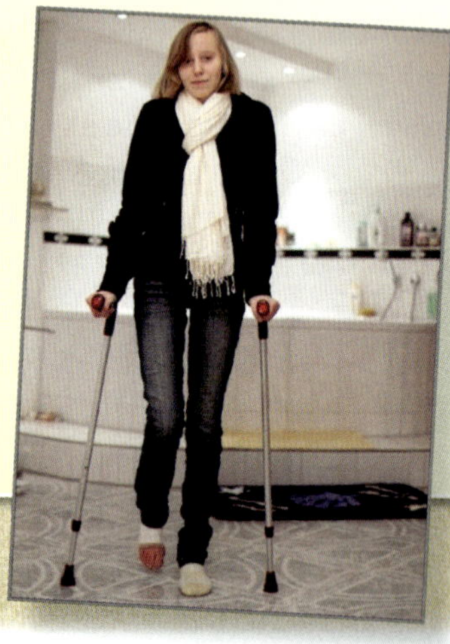

1 What's the name of the class teacher?
2 What happened to Sally?
3 How long is she going to be away from school?
4 What is the teacher going to send her?
5 What is the big news?

4 **Imagine one of your classmates is at home and can't come to school. Write him or her a letter. Think about the questions above to help you with ideas.**

Check your progress Units 7 and 8

1 Write the names of the sports.

1 ....

2 ....

3 ....

4 ....

5 ....

6 ....

6

2 Complete the words for sicknesses.

1 st _ _ _ _ _ ache
2 e_ _ ache
3 a s _ _ _ th _ _ _ _
4 a c _ _ _
5 t _ _ _ _ ache
6 to feel d _ _ _ _

6

3 Complete the dialogue using the correct form of the past continuous.

A What [1]........................ Sarah .... (do) last night?
B She [2]........................ (work) at my house. We [3]........................ (do) our homework together.
A [4]........................ you .... (study) for the biology test?
B Yes, we [5]........................ !

5

4 Complete the sentences with a time preposition.

1 .... Monday, I went to see my brother.
2 We went on vacation .... July last year.
3 The movie started .... 7:00 p.m.
4 I saw them .... night.
5 It began .... 1974.
6 I went swimming .... the morning.
7 We sleep .... night.
8 My birthday is .... November 1.

8

5 Complete the text with the superlative form.

The [1].................. (interesting) thing about me is my hair. It's red and curly and very long. Sometimes I think it's the [2].................. (bad) hair in the world because it's always messy, but sometimes I think it's the [3].................. (good) hair in the world because I look different and people talk to me a lot. I know this boy named Mark. He's the [4].................. (tall) boy in school and the [5].................. (intelligent). He always talks to me because he thinks my hair is great.

5

6 Complete the dialogue using the present continuous and the correct form of the verb *to be*.

A [1]......................... (you/go) to your cousin's house tomorrow?
B Yes, we [2]......................... . We [3]......................... (see) a movie.
A [4]......................... (you/stay) there all weekend?
B No, we [5]......................... . We [6]......................... (go) to the country on Sunday.
A What [7]......................... (you/do) there?
B We [8]......................... (visit) my grandmother.
A [9]......................... (she/meet) you at your cousin's?
B No, my aunt [10]......................... (come) to get us.

10

7 Write five sentences about what you were doing at six o'clock last night and at eight o'clock this morning.

10

TOTAL 50

My progress so far is ...

- great! ☐
- good. ☐
- poor. ☐

Sports in the United States

1 Match the sport to the correct picture.

1 baseball
2 football
3 basketball

5 **2 Take the quiz, and then listen and check your answers.**

Do you know?

Baseball is a mixture of the English games rounders and cricket, while football is a mixture of the games soccer and rugby.

An American SPORTS QUIZ!

1 Which sport is the oldest?
a football
b basketball
c baseball

2 Which sport do these terms come from: pitcher, home run, and pennant?
a baseball
b football
c rounders

3 There are... players in a baseball team.
a 9 b 11 c 13

4 The tallest basketball player is a Romanian, Gheorghe Muresan of the Washington Bullets. He is... .
a 2.31 m
b 2.20 m
c 2 m

5 What is a baseball field called?
a a star
b a diamond
c a square

6 The Cincinnati Red Stockings were the first professional ... team.
a basketball
b baseball
c football

7 How many points do you score for a touchdown in football?
a 5 b 6 c 1

3 Read and complete the table below.

My sports hero is Michael Jordan. He is the best basketball player in the history of the game. He joined the Chicago Bulls after he left college. The Chicago Bulls won three NBA championships with him on the team, and they had 72 wins in one season.

My sports hero is Joe DiMaggio. He was a famous baseball player. He died in 1999. He played for the New York Yankees. They won nine world championships with him on the team.

My sports hero is Joe Montana. He is a famous American football player. He was a quarterback for the San Francisco 49ers. His nickname is Joe Cool. In 1981, the 49ers won the NFC title with Joe on the team, and they defeated Cincinnati 26–21 in the Super Bowl.

NAME	TEAM	WINS
Joe DiMaggio	New York Yankees	Nine World Championships
		26–21 (against Cincinnati)
		3 NBA Championships

4 Over 2 U! Complete a table for your sports hero and write a short paragraph about that person.

MORE! Now you can watch Episode 4 of *Kids in NYC!* DVD

The world of birds
the biggest and the smallest

Ostriches

Ostriches are native to Africa, but they can live pretty much anywhere. They are the biggest birds in the world and normally are about 2.5 meters tall, so it isn't surprising that ostrich eggs are the biggest eggs in the world! An ostrich egg weighs about 1.6 kilograms, or about the same as 24 chicken eggs. In 1997, in Shanxi, China, an ostrich laid the heaviest egg in the world. It weighed 2.35 kilograms! The female ostrich sits on its egg in the daytime, and the male sits on it at night. The baby ostrich comes out of the egg after about 40 days.

Ostriches are also the fastest birds on land in the world. They can run at about 72 kilometers an hour. Ostriches are sometimes dangerous. They have very strong feet and can attack animals and people. Ostriches usually live between 50 and 75 years.

Bee hummingbirds

Bee hummingbirds live in Cuba. The males are the smallest birds in the world, while the female bee hummingbird is slightly bigger than the male. The male bee hummingbird weighs only 1.8 grams. That's lighter than a penny! The male is about five centimeters long.

When it is flying, the bee hummingbird moves its wings between 80 and 200 times every second. It has the highest body temperature of all birds in the world: about 40°C in the daytime, and about 20°C at night. Its body temperature goes down at night to save energy. Every day, a bee hummingbird eats about one gram of food (half its weight) and drinks about 15 grams of water (about eight times its weight!). Bee hummingbirds mostly eat insects and the nectar they get from flowers.

For MORE! Go to www.more-online.com/american and take a quiz on this text.

UNIT 9

Guess what?

In this unit

You learn

- past continuous vs. simple past
- *one/ones*
- quantity *a lot of, much, many*
- words for emotions

and then you can

- give reasons
- talk about emotions

6 **1 Listen and read.**

Tony Guess what just happened?

Sally What?

Tony I was walking down Maple Street when I saw two lights. They were on a huge silver thing that was blocking the street. Then a door opened and a lot of men came out. They were wearing silver clothing and had masks on their faces. The tallest one came up to me and said, "Why are you here?" I said, "I'm here because I live around here." But he asked me again, "Why are you here?" I wanted to run away, but the other ones blocked my path. The tall one said, "Send him away. There are not many more streets left and we haven't got much time."

Harry To do what? Catch people like you? What's this all about? Aliens?

Tony Maybe. They're still out there. Why don't you check?

(A minute later)

Harry Hilarious, Tony. Your aliens are people from the gas company, looking for a gas leak.

Tony Gotcha!

2 **Put a check next to the correct answer.**

1 Tony was walking down
- ☐ Maple Street.
- ☐ Sixth Avenue.
- ☐ Main Street.

2 A huge silver thing
- ☐ crashed into a tree.
- ☐ was going past him.
- ☐ was blocking the street.

3 The tallest person came up to Tony and said
- ☐ "Leave us alone!"
- ☐ "We want to take over the world."
- ☐ "Why are you here?"

4 Tony asks Harry to
- ☐ go with him to the spaceship.
- ☐ go outside to see for himself.
- ☐ help him against the aliens.

5 The people in silver are from
- ☐ the gas company.
- ☐ another planet.
- ☐ another country.

Get talking Giving reasons

7 **3** **Listen and repeat.**

A Why weren't you at school?
B Because I had a cold.

A Why were you on the Internet for an hour?
B Because I had to answer 50 emails.

4 **Match the questions and answers. Then work with a partner and act out the dialogues.**

1 Why didn't you come to the park?
2 Why weren't you at Sue's party?
3 Why don't you watch the movie?
4 Why didn't you go swimming?

a Because it was too cold.
b Because I think it's boring.
c Because I was too tired.
d Because I had toothache.

Language Focus

Vocabulary Emotions

8 **1** **Listen and write the number of the correct word on the left in the picture.**

1 happy
2 nervous
3 shocked
4 surprised
5 scared
6 frightened
7 sad
8 thrilled
9 angry
10 bored

Get talking Talking about emotions

2 **Work with a partner. Talk about how you feel in these situations:**

When I get a good score on a test, I feel happy.

- You get a good score on a test.
- You meet up with a friend after a long time.
- You win a lot of money.
- You listen to a long speech.
- You lose a game.
- You have an exam.

Grammar

Past continuous vs. simple past

1 **Complete the sentence below with the verbs in the correct tense. Check against the dialogue on page 84.**

I [1]................................. down Maple Street when I [2]................................. two lights. (walk/see)

A longer action (**past continuous**) is interrupted by a shorter one (**simple past**).
They ***were having*** a picnic when they ***heard*** a noise.

2 **Circle the correct verb form.**

1 James *made* / *was making* coffee when we came into the kitchen.
2 When she broke her ankle she *played* / *was playing* volleyball.
3 Joanna *listened* / *was listening* to music when I came into her room.
4 I *rode* / *was riding* my bike when someone called my name.
5 When *we met* / *were meeting* her, she was crying.
6 When *you saw* / *were seeing* me, I was running.

3 **Complete the sentences with the past continuous and the simple past tense.**

1 When it started to rain, I was working in the yard. (start / work)
2 I .... a show on TV when he .... me. (watch / call)
3 They .... to Rita when I .... (talk / arrive)
4 When James .... , we .... dinner. (call / have)
5 Tamara .... emails when the lights .... out. (write /go)
6 I .... on the phone when I suddenly .... a loud noise. (talk / hear)
7 Kate and Rick .... when someone .... Kate's purse. (dance / steal)

They were having a picnic in the backyard when they heard a noise!

4 **Work with a partner. Ask her/him what she/he was doing at different times during the weekend.**

A What were you doing on Sunday at 3:00 p.m.?
B I was listening to music. What were you doing on Saturday at 8:00 p.m.?
A I was at the mall with my mom.

one / ones

5 **Look at the examples. Which words do *one* and *ones* replace?**

A Which boy are you talking about?
B The **one** with the black cap.

A Would you like the red or the blue sneakers?
B The red **ones** please.

6 **Complete the dialogue with the words below. Listen and check. Then act it out.**

9

large one | the blue one | one (x2)

Richard Dad? Can I have different T-shirt?
Dad Why? What's wrong with that [1]................................... ?
Richard Nothing, but I want my extra [2]................................... ;
[3]................................... that has an alien's head on it.
Dad Sorry, I can't give you that [4]...................................
Richard Why not?
Dad I washed it, and the water was too hot.
Now it's extra small!

Quantity *a lot of / much / many*

7 **Look at the examples and complete the rules below.**

There were **a lot of** men. We don't have **much (a lot of)** time left.
There was **a lot of** rain in May. There weren't **many (a lot of)** people at the concert.

1 We use [1]... with count and noncount nouns in the affirmative and negative form.

2 We use [2]... with noncount nouns in the negative form.

3 We use [3]... with count nouns in the negative form.

8 **Complete the sentences with *much* or *many*.**

1 **A** Can you give me some money, please?
B Sorry, I don't have .... myself.
2 When I was in Boston last Christmas, there wasn't .... snow.
3 John doesn't have .... friends.
4 My doctor says I shouldn't put .... salt on my food.

Skills

Reading

1 **Read the story.**

A NEW HOME PART 1

THE PRESIDENT OF TROJAN

The president of the planet Trojan was standing in front of her palace. She spoke to all the people.

"People of Trojan!" she said. "I have some bad news. Another planet is coming toward us. 100 years from now, the other planet is going to hit us and destroy us. There is nothing we can do."

The Trojan people were very scared. The president said more.

"Don't worry. We've got a plan. We're going to build spaceships, the biggest spaceships in the history of the universe. Each spaceship is going to carry 10,000 people, and we are going to build 20,000 spaceships! In this way, we can take every Trojan man, woman, and child to a safe place before the other planet hits us."

The people asked, "Where? Where is this safe place?"

The president said, "There is another planet, very far from here. It is a planet where Trojan people can live. The air is like our air, the water is like our water, and there is room for us. The name of this planet is Earth!"

The next day, the people of Trojan started to build the spaceships. It took them a very long time (more than fifteen years) to build the first 1,000 spaceships. And after 50 years, 5,000 spaceships were ready. Finally, all 20,000 spaceships were ready. The spaceships were round, like huge yellow footballs. They were so big that 10,000 Trojans could fit inside each one.

Then, one day, the people of Trojan said good-bye to their home. They got into their spaceships. And, one by one, the spaceships took off. The Trojans began the journey to their new home.

20 years later, the spaceships landed on the planet Earth.

2 **Match the sentence halves.**

1 Another planet was going to...	a into each spaceship.
2 The Trojan people planned...	b 20,000 very big spaceships.
3 The Trojan people built...	c hit the planet Trojan.
4 10,000 Trojan people went...	d on planet Earth.
5 After 20 years, the Trojan people landed...	e to travel to Earth.

Listening

10 **3** **Listen to the end of the story and put the pictures in order.**

11 **4** **Listen again and choose the correct answers.**

1 Jenny's dog barked because he saw:
  a strange yellow seeds.
  b a cat.
  c Jenny's father.

2 Jenny's father thought the seeds were:
  a strange.
  b beautiful.
  c dirty.

3 Jenny put the seeds:
  a in the house.
  b in her father's car.
  c in the garbage can.

Speaking and listening

5 **Work in pairs. Use the words and pictures to tell the story.**

key
a strange green light
a strange noise
lock
turn around
pick up

12 **6** **Listen to the story.**

Reading and speaking

7 **Here are two possibilities for the next part of the story. Choose which one you like best and say why.**

A

James went into the house. He saw a chair and he sat down. It was very comfortable! Then he found a button on the floor, near the chair. "What's this?" he said, and he pushed the button. The chair started to go around and around very quickly, but after a minute it stopped. James went out of the house. He was in the year 2090!

B

James went into the house. He saw a chair and he sat down. It was very comfortable! He went to sleep.

Five hours later, James woke up. In front of him were two strange people with pink eyes. "Why are you here?" said one of the strange people. "You shouldn't be here! Now we have to take you to our planet!"

I like the first one better because it's...

Writing for your Portfolio

8 **Write your own end to the story.**

James went into the house. He saw a chair and he sat down...

9 **Work in groups of four. Tell your stories and decide whose story you like best.**

MORE fun with Fido

Famous modern authors for teenagers

Key words

famous author	sell books	publish a book
journalist	popular book	translation
win prizes	publisher	invent a story / novel

1 **Read the fact files about three famous authors who write for teenagers.**

FACT FILE

Name: Jacqueline Wilson
Born: 1945, Bath, England.
Other jobs before writing: Journalist
Wrote first novel: 1954 (aged nine)
Famous novels: *Double Act, Vicky Angel, Girls in Love, Tracy Beaker.*
Interesting fact: She has more than 15,000 books in her house!

FACT FILE

Name: Eoin Colfer
Born: 1965, Wexford, Ireland.
Other jobs before writing: Elementary school teacher
Wrote first novel: 1999
Famous novels: *Benny and Omar, Artemis Fowl.*
Interesting fact: He has worked in Saudi Arabia, Tunisia, and Italy.

FACT FILE

Name: Jerry Spinelli
Born: 1941, Pennsylvania, USA
Other jobs before writing: Editor
Wrote first novel: 1982
Famous novels: *Maniac Magee*
Interesting fact: He wanted to be a baseball player. When he was 16, he wrote a poem about a football game. His local newspaper published it!

2 **Read the summaries of three novels. Which book would you like to read?**

Vicky Angel **by Jacqueline Wilson**
Jade and Vicky have been best friends since kindergarten. One day the two girls argue. The same day Vicky gets killed by a car. Jade cannot forget Vicky. She tries to make new friends. But one day Vicky appears again as a ghost. Jade is happy, but other people see that she's talking to herself and they think she's crazy. Jade goes and sees a psychologist who helps her to find out who she really is.

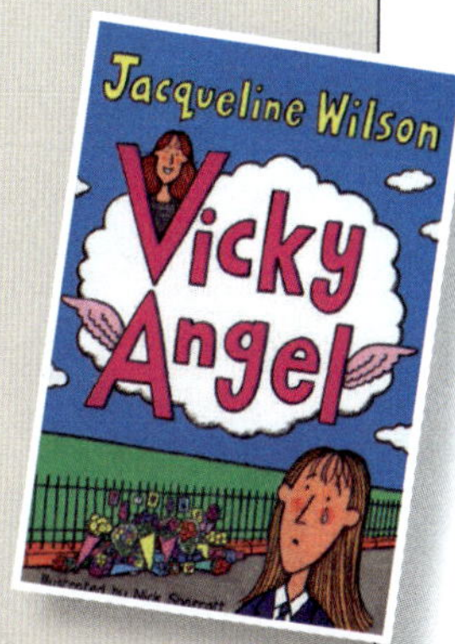

Maniac Magee **by Jerry Spinelli**
Jeffrey "Maniac" Magee is a young white boy whose parents die in an accident. Jeffrey starts to live with his aunt and uncle, but he soon runs away from home and lives for some time in a zoo. Then a black family takes him in. Jeffrey soon finds out that there is a problem. In the town there are black people who live in the East End and white people who live in the West End. Jeffrey doesn't understand why the blacks and whites do not like each other. He travels throughout the town and tries to change how the people think.

Artemis Fowl **by Eoin Colfer**
Artemis Fowl is 12 years old. The Fowls are an old Irish family. Artemis wants to get rich. He finds out that fairies and elves exist and that they have magical books. He plans to get one. He hopes that the book will show him how to get the gold treasure of the fairies. With the help of his butler he tricks an old fairy woman. She lends him her magical book but only for 30 minutes. Artemis scans it with a digital camera and emails it to his computer. He tries to find out about the treasure of the fairies. But he needs help so he kidnaps an elf. A big fight begins.

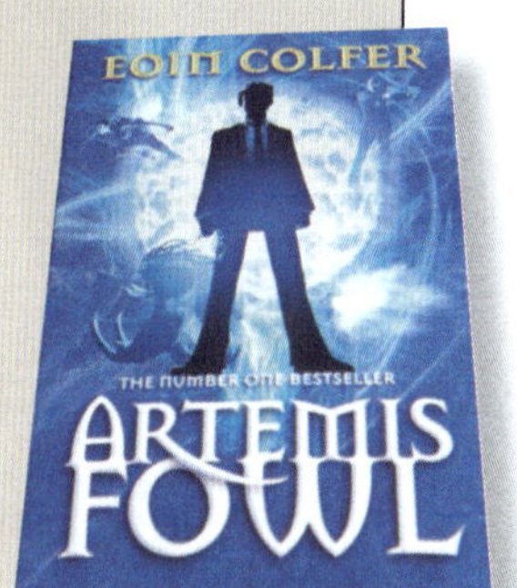

I think … sounds interesting/boring/funny.

I like /don't like stories about …

Mini Project Authors and books

3

Either
Check the Internet or the library to discover facts about a writer for teens.

Scott Westerfeld is an American science fiction writer. His books are for young adults...

Or
Write a short summary of a book that you have read and enjoyed.

A book that I really enjoyed was The Catcher in the Rye by J.D. Salinger. It was published in 1951. It tells the story of a 16-year-old boy named Holden Caulfield...

UNIT 10 Shouldn't we ask?

In this unit

You learn
- *should/shouldn't*
- conjunctions: *and/so/but/because*
- words for directions and places

and then you can
- use large numbers
- give advice
- ask for and give directions

13 **1 Listen and read.**

Sally Let's ask someone again.
Harry No way! I hate asking for directions. Let me look at the map.
Olivia Come on. Shouldn't we ask? We're lost.
Harry We're not. I can figure this out.
Sally Look. I'll give you one minute to figure it out because I'm getting really tired.
Harry OK. We're here at the corner of Market Street and Cooper Lane. If we turn right at the end of Cooper Lane and then take the second left, we are close to the gas station.
Sally Yes, there's the gas station on the map. And from there?
Olivia I think we should ask somebody now.
Harry Hang on. From the gas station we walk straight on as far as the post office. There we turn left again. And then… we're lost again, so, let's start over.
Olivia Let's ask someone!
Sally Excuse me, where's the movie theater?
Officer Just cross the street and turn right. It's there!
Sally Thanks! Come on Harry!

2 **Circle T (True) or F (False) for the sentences below.**

1 Harry wants to look at the map. T / F
2 Olivia wants to ask for directions. T / F
3 They are at the corner of Cooper Lane and Main Street. T / F
4 Harry says they have to go to the end of Cooper Lane. T / F
5 They're looking for the post office. T / F
6 The movie theater is very close. T / F

Get talking Using large numbers

14 **3** **Listen and repeat.**

100 one hundred
1,000 one thousand
100,000 one hundred thousand
1,000,000 one million

8,347 eight thousand, three hundred, and forty-seven
47,222 forty-seven thousand, two hundred, and twenty-two
721,877 seven hundred and twenty-one thousand, eight hundred, and seventy-seven

15 **4** **Now say these numbers. Then listen and check.**

9,341	52,304	72,605	823,988	1,000,732

5 **Work with a partner. Use the picture and talk about saving money.**

A How much did Jane save this year?

B She saved $1,204.

Language Focus

Vocabulary Directions and places

16 **1 Listen and repeat.**

go straight ahead

turn left

turn right

take the second right

take the first left

go past the…

cross the…

go as far as the…

17 **2 Match the places to the correct numbers. Then listen and check.**

☐ gas station
☐ parking lot
☐ school
☐ post office
☐ tourist office
☐ bank
☐ hospital
☐ movie theater
☐ grocery store
☐ restaurant
☐ hotel

Get talking Asking for and giving directions

18 **3 Listen and repeat.**

A Where's the post office?
B Go straight ahead and take the second left.

A How do I get to a gas station?
B Go straight ahead and take the first left.

4 Work with a partner. Choose different places from Exercise 2 and give directions from X.

Grammar

Should/shouldn't

1 **Look at the dialogue on page 94 and complete the examples.**

I think we [1].. ask someone now.
[2].. we ask?

We use ***should*** and ***shouldn't*** to give advice and to say what we think is a good idea.
Should is the same for all subjects (***I/you/he*** etc.). It is followed by the base form of the verb.

2 **Match the sentences to make dialogues.**

1 I'm tired.
2 I have a headache.
3 My teacher's angry with me.
4 My cat's sick.
5 It's raining outside.
6 It's a dangerous part of town.

a You shouldn't talk in class.
b You should take it to the vet.
c You should take an umbrella.
d You shouldn't go there alone.
e You shouldn't go to bed so late.
f You should take an aspirin.

3 **Complete the sentences with *should* or *shouldn't*.**

1 **A** I don't feel very well.
B You .... go to bed.

2 **A** We're bored.
B You .... watch so much TV.

3 **A** There's a new girl at school named Gillian.
B You .... invite her to our barbecue.

4 **A** I don't understand my math homework.
B You .... ask your teacher to explain it again.

5 **A** I can't fall asleep at night.
B You .... drink so much caffeine.

6 **A** I don't have any money.
B You .... buy so much music.

7 **A** I'm going to live in Brazil for a year.
B You .... learn some Portuguese.

8 **A** I failed my science test.
B You .... study more.

4 **Work in pairs. Say what these people *should* and *shouldn't* do. Use the words below.**

clean his room do his homework call a friend listen to music
talk on his cell phone rent a DVD watch TV read

Conjunctions *and / so / but / because*

5 **Match the sentence halves. Check against the dialogue on page 94.**

I know the store is on King Street, **but**	I'm getting tired.
Just cross the street **and**	I can't find it at the moment.
And then ... we're lost again, **so**	turn right.
I'll only give you one minute to figure it out **because**	let's start over.

6 **Match the sentence halves.**

1 I looked for the key,
2 My friends were sick
3 I got a high score on the test
4 The movie started at 10,
5 She likes you a lot
6 I thought I had some money,

a and had to stay at home.
b because I had studied really hard.
c so we couldn't be home by 11 o'clock.
d so I couldn't buy anything.
e but I couldn't find it.
f because she thinks you are so smart.

They wanted to go swimming, but it was too cold!

7 **Complete the dialogue in the sentences below. Listen and check, and then act the dialogue out.**

19

she gave us directions	we went home
they were for the wrong theater	we couldn't find the theater

Dana Hi Jim, did you enjoy the movie last night?
Jim We didn't see it because [1]..
Dana Why didn't you ask someone the way?
Jim Well, we asked someone and [2]..
Dana So what was the problem?
Jim She gave us directions, but [3]..
Dana The wrong theater? What did you do?
Jim We didn't want to see the movie that was on there, so [4]..

Skills

Reading

1 **Read the dialogues and write the letter of the correct building in the signs.**

Post office

Restaurant

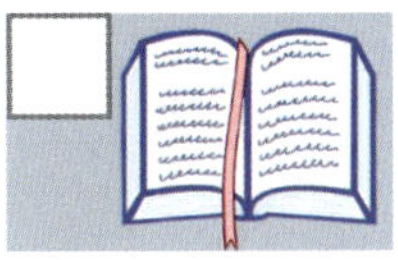
Library

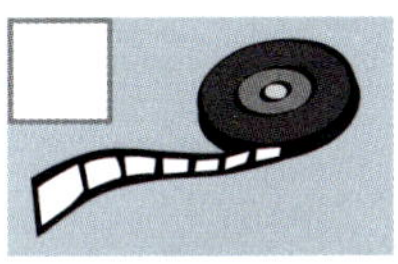
Movie theater

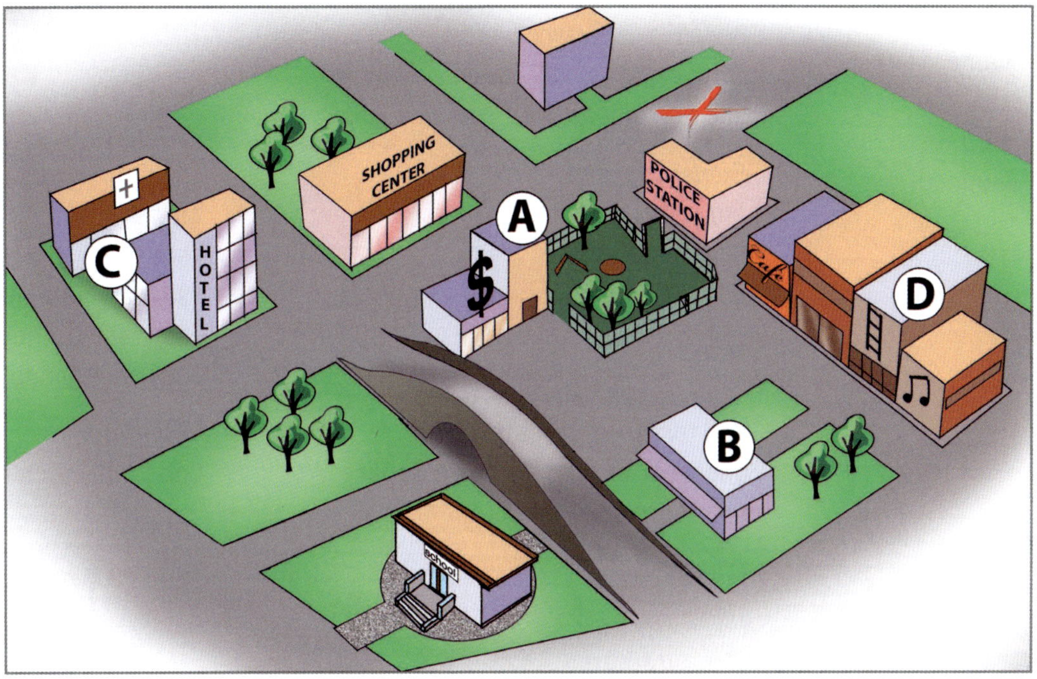

Dialogue 1:

Woman Excuse me, where's the post office?

Man Go straight ahead as far as the grocery store. Then turn left. On the corner, there's a large bank. The post office is next to the bank.

Woman Thank you.

Man You're welcome.

Dialogue 2:

Boy Excuse me. Can you tell me where the movie theater is?

Woman The theater? It's on Hill Street.

Boy How do I get there?

Woman Go straight ahead, take the first left, and go past the police station. You'll see a little park in front of you. Go past the park and straight ahead and the theater is next door to a large music shop.

Boy Thank you.

Woman No problem.

Listening

20 **2** **Listen to two more dialogues and write the letters of the other two buildings on the signs.**

A Song 4 U Looking for Liz

21 **3** **Listen and complete the song with the words on the left.**

went
know
go
far
name
see
stop
laughed

Chorus
Young man:
I'm looking for my friend,
I don't [1]........ where she is.
I'm looking for my friend,
she has blonde hair, her [2]........ is Liz.

Excuse me, sir?
Did you [3]........ her?
Where did she [4]........ ?
I have to know.

Man 1:
She [5]........ along Main Street,
and turned right at the store.
She went as [6]........ as Town Square
And there I saw her stop.

Chorus

Man 1:
I saw her [7]........ at Town Square.
I saw a young man wait for her.
They talked. They [8]........ .
They said goodbye.

Young man:
Can I still catch her?

Man 1:
You can try.

Writing for your Portfolio

4 **Write a similar email with directions from school to your house.**

To: Josh	**From:** Sally	**Re:** Directions to my house
Go straight ahead from the school. Take the first right and then the second left and that's my street, 104th Street. I'm at 3955.		

Check your progress Units 9 and 10

1 Complete the words about emotions.

1 When I gave my presentation, I was very n _ _ _ _ _ _.
2 I was sh _ _ _ _ _ when I failed the test.
3 He was t _ _ _ _ _ _ _ _ when he won the race.
4 They were a _ _ _ _ when they lost all their money.
5 She was s _ _ _ _ _ to be in the house all alone.
6 I was s _ _ _ _ _ _ _ _ when she didn't come.

6

2 Write the direction words.

1 .... 2 .... 3 ....

4 .... 5 .... 6 ....

6

3 Complete the text. Use the simple past or the past continuous.

I [1]...................... (walk) down the street yesterday when I [2]......................(hear) a strange noise. I [3]...................... (look) down and [4]......................(see) a strange green man. He [5]...................... (run) down the street in front of me. "Stop!" I [6]...................... (shout). He didn't hear me, so I [7]......................(run) after him into the park. In front of me there was a big crowd of small yellow people. They [8].................. (talk) and [9]...................... (dance). I [10].................. (start) to dance, too! Suddenly, a loud voice said, "Wake up Tom!" I [11]...................... (open) my eyes and my friend Sam [12]...................... (stand) next to me. "You [13]...................... (dance) in your sleep!" he said.

13

4 Complete the sentences with *a lot of, much,* or *many*.

1 This room is very dark. There isn't .... light in it.
2 There wasn't .... time.
3 There weren't .... things to do there.
4 There was .... traffic this morning. It was terrible!
5 There weren't .... books in the store.

5

5 Complete the sentences with *and, so, but,* or *because*.

1 I didn't feel well, ... I stayed at home.
2 He liked her .... she was happy.
3 I went to Spain, ... I wanted to go home.
4 She likes swimming .... jogging.
5 We were late .... there was an accident.

5

6 Complete with *the one* or *the ones*.

A Can I try on those jeans?
B [1].............. in the window?
A No, [2].............. here. Oh, and that T-shirt, too.
B [3].............. near the window?
A No, [4].............. over there.
B Sure! Those jeans are nice, too. [5].............. with the silver stars.

5

7 Write advice for a friend who is bored / not ready / nervous about an exam or sad / angry with his / her parents.

10

TOTAL 50

My progress so far is ...

great! ☐
good. ☐
poor. ☐

Learn MORE about Culture

The history of the car

1 **Read about the history of the car.**

In the 1700s, a Frenchman named Antoine de la Mothe Cadillac went to the United States and founded the city of Detroit. Many years later, in 1902, an engineer named his car after the Frenchman. The famous Cadillac is still a very popular car today.

In 1896, Henry Ford built the first American gas-powered car in Detroit. He called it the Quadricycle because it was made with four bicycle wheels. He also produced the first cheap car there, the Model T Ford. In the same year, William Durrant founded General Motors, and Detroit became the Motor City of America.

Do YOU know?

The earliest cars were very uncomfortable. The driver's seat and the front seat of the car was a hard bench.

Cars were definitely not fast. In 1898, the New York City Police Department chased speeding motorists on bicycles.

In the early 1900s when Henry Ford produced the first gas-powered cars in the United States, there was only one color, BLACK.

2 **Match the cars with the model.**

1 Cadillac 2 Model T 3 Mustang

A ____

B ____

C ____

3 **Which car is it? Guess the answers. Then listen and check.**

22

Silver Ghost Fiat Ferrari

1 The first .... was built in 1899 in Italy. Its top speed was 35 kilometers per hour. Only 25 of them were produced.
2 From 1906 until 1922 there was one model of this luxury car. It was the .... The owner of this company loved flying. He died in a plane crash in 1910, before his cars became successful.
3 The owner of this company was a racing driver and the first .... was a racing car. Later, in 1948, the company built the first sports cars for the road.

4 **Over 2 U!** **Find out about a kind of car that you like. Write a brief description of it and its history.**

MORE! **Now you can watch Episode 5 of *Kids in NYC!*** DVD

Looking for Keiko

Last year a Japanese girl stayed at our house. Her name was Keiko, and she was here with her classmates and her English teacher.

Keiko was not very good at finding her way around so Dad took her everywhere in the car. One day he didn't have time, so he asked me to meet Keiko at school, but I forgot.

I was in my room when the phone rang. It was Keiko. "Hello" she said, "I am lost. I don't know where I am. Can you help me?"

I was in trouble! I could hear Dad saying, "What did I tell you, George? Go and meet Keiko at school! No video games for the rest of the week, young man!"

"Of course!" I said. "Where are you?"

"I don't know," she said. "There are a lot of gray houses, and they all look the same. And there's a bus stop at the end of the street."

"Keiko," I said. "Listen. What's the name of the street?"

"I don't know. I can't see a street sign."

"Walk to the corner, Keiko," I said. "There should be a sign."

"Oh, yes, I can see it. Hello? My battery's low."

"Keiko," I shouted. "Just tell me the name of the street. And stay where you are!"

"Yes, the name of the street is very long. It's …"

Just then there was a click. I couldn't believe it!

I put on my jacket and got my bike. I thought, "She walked from the school, so maybe she walked in this direction from there."

I went back to the school and then followed the main route back to my house. Half an hour later there was still no Keiko. I rode my bike back home. I went up and down some smaller roads. Still no Keiko.

About 200 meters away from my house, there's a street up a long hill. I didn't want to go up that street, but then I thought: "OK, I may as well..." I turned onto the street. Then I checked out the side streets. First left—nothing. Second, third, fourth left—nothing. I was so tired. First right—and just 100 meters away, there was Keiko. I waved and called her name. She saw and ran up to me. She was so happy to see me.

I was happy to see her, too!

For MORE! Go to www.more-online.com/american and do a quiz on this text.

UNIT 11 It won't rain

In this unit

You learn
- *will/ won't*
- *might/might (not)*
- words for the weather

and then you can
- make excuses
- talk about the weather

23 **1 Listen and read.**

Sally Hi, Fred. It's Sally! We're going to the beach this afternoon. Would you like to come?
Fred I'm not sure. I think it might rain.
Sally Really? Look outside—the sky's blue, there aren't any clouds, and there's not even a breeze. It won't rain. No way!
Fred OK, I'll be there in 10 minutes.
(*Harry comes in*)
Harry Who was that?
Sally Fred. He'll be here in 10 minutes. He thinks going to the beach might not be a good idea. It might rain!
(10 minutes later)
Fred Are you sure you want to go to the beach?
Sally Of course. It'll be hot and sunny for the rest of the day.
Fred Too hot! I think there might be a thunderstorm. Why don't we stay here and watch a DVD?
Sally Oh Fred, not again! I don't want to watch DVDs three times a week.

2 **Circle T (True) or F (False) for the sentences below.**

1 Sally and Harry want to go to the beach in the afternoon. T / F
2 Fred thinks it might rain. T / F
3 There are some clouds in the sky. T / F
4 Sally thinks the weather will be good for the rest of the day. T / F
5 Fred thinks there might be a thunderstorm. T / F
6 Sally wants to watch a DVD. T / F

Get talking Making excuses

24 **3** **Listen and number.**

4 **Work with a partner and match the phrases. Then make dialogues.**

1 Let's go to the park.
2 Let's ride our bikes.
3 Let's go to a movie.
4 Let's go skateboarding.
5 Let's go and buy some candy.

a No, there might be a lot of people there.
b No, there might not be any tickets left.
c No, I might get a toothache.
d No, it might rain soon.
e No, I might get hurt.

Language Focus

Vocabulary Weather words

25 **1** **Write the correct numbers in the pictures. Then listen and check.**

1 sunny 3 rainy / showers 5 snowy 7 thunderstorms 9 cold
2 windy 4 cloudy 6 foggy 8 hot

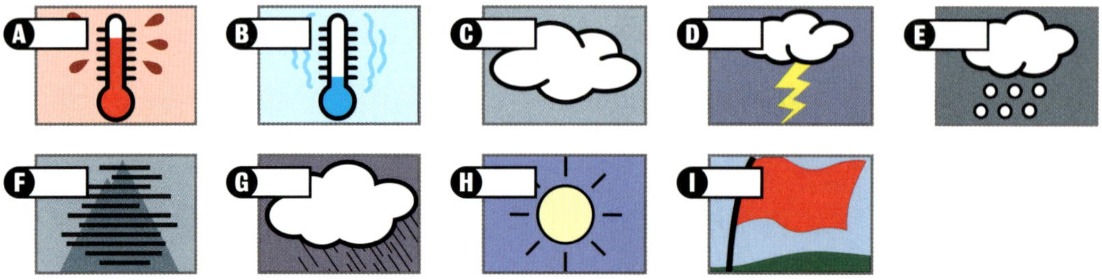

Get talking Talking about the weather

26 **2** **Listen and repeat.**

A What's the weather like in Seattle?
B It's very rainy and windy.

A What's the weather like in Boston?
B It's foggy and cold and only 12°C.

3 **Work with a partner. Take turns to describe the weather and guess the place.**

A It's very windy and rainy here and only 14°C.

B You're in Seattle.

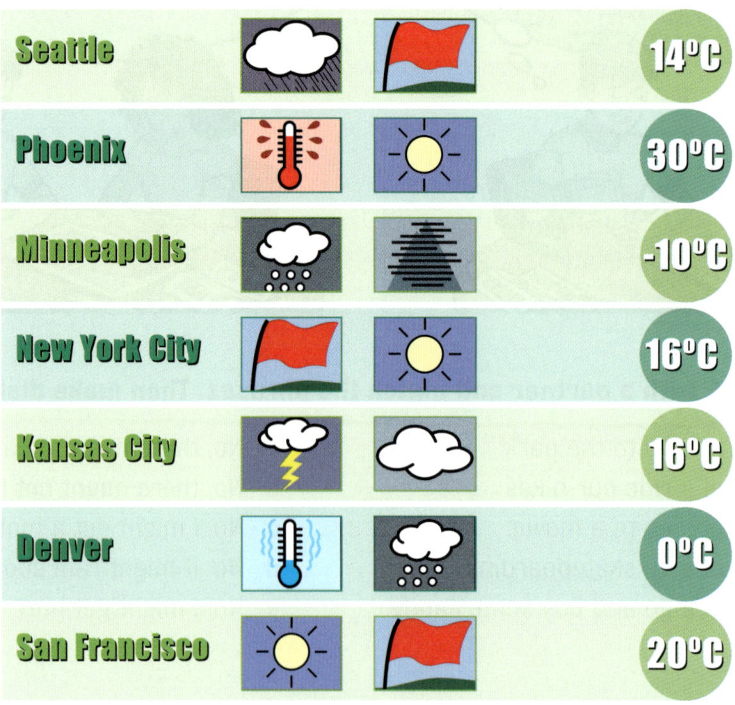

Grammar

Will / won't

1 Look at the dialogue on page 104 and complete the examples.

He [1].......... be here in 10 minutes.
It [2]..................... rain. No way!
I [3]..................... be there in 10 minutes.

We use ***will*** and ***won't*** for expectation, hopes, and predictions for the future.
Will and ***won't*** are the same for all subjects (**I/you/he,** etc.). They are followed by the base form of the verb.
We **will meet** again. (We**'ll meet** again.)
I **will not be** away for a very long time. (I **won't be** away for a very long time.)

We also use the *will* future when we spontaneously make a decision, promise, or offer.
Maybe **I'll try** cooking, too.
I'll help you with your homework tonight.

2 Put the words in the correct order to make sentences. Use short forms.

1 it / rain / I / tomorrow / think / will
I think it'll rain tomorrow.
2 soon / sister / car/ buy / will / a / my
....
3 thunderstorm / be / this / will not / afternoon / a / there /
....
4 win / race / will not / you / the /
....
5 they / year / will / go / to New York / next
....
6 year / move / he / next / will
....
7 you / I / shopping / go / will / for
....
8 will not / much / time. / I / have
....

Will Questions and short answers

Questions	**Will** I / you / she / he / it / we / you / they be famous?
Short answers	Yes, I / you / she / he / it / we / you / they **will**. No, I / you / she / he / it / we / you / they **won't**.

3 Write questions for these answers.

1 No, my friends won't go to the beach tomorrow.
Will your friends go to the beach tomorrow?
2 Yes, the sun will come out soon.
....?
3 Yes, I will be here later.
....?
4 Yes, we will stay here for the weekend.
....?
5 No, they won't go out tonight.
....?

Might / might not

4 **Complete the examples with the missing words. Then check against the dialogue on page 104.**

He thinks going to the beach [1]......... .... be a good idea.
I think there [2]......... be a thunderstorm.

We use ***might*** and ***might not*** to talk about possibility or uncertainty in the future.
Might is the same for all subjects (***I/you/he,*** etc.). It is followed by the base form of the verb.

5 **Complete with *might* or *might not*.**

1 I'm tired. I might go to bed early tonight.
2 He left the office very late, so he .... be home for dinner.
3 There are a lot of clouds in the sky, so it .... rain later.
4 She didn't pass her test, so she .... be very happy.
5 They're a good team. They .... win the championship this year.

6 **Read the story. Complete the speech bubbles with the numbers of the correct phrases.**

1 I have too much to do.
2 The test has been postponed.
3 We might get home too late.
4 We're going to a movie.

7 **Read William's worries. Work with a partner and think of his reasons to worry.**

1 I don't want to go to the beach. — It might be too hot.
2 I don't want to go skiing. — ....
3 I don't want to go near that dog. — ....

Skills

Reading

1 **Read and match the texts to the correct photo.**

1

Jo

Last year, I went on vacation in California. We visited Joshua Tree National Park. We went in May and it was very HOT! There were some strange rock formations. They were like nothing I'd ever seen before. There were also the most amazing trees. They are the Joshua trees after which the park is named.

2
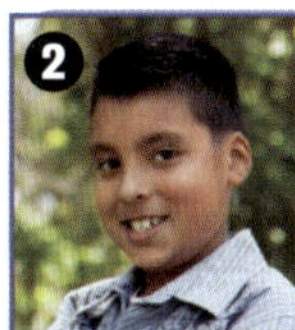
Juan

I went to Las Vegas, Nevada, last summer and it was very, very hot. There were never any clouds in the sky! It was more than 30 degrees every day until about 8:00 p.m.! I liked it, but this summer I think we'll go somewhere different — somewhere a little colder!

3

Mel

To me, the Boundary Waters that lie between the United States and Canada is the most beautiful place in the world. I went there over the summer last year. But it's not the warmest place to go. The water is freezing, so I think I'll go to Mexico this year!

4

Linda

Last spring my family and I went to Vancouver and stayed at my aunt's house during spring break. It rained almost the entire time and the house was very cold, especially upstairs! But there are some cool places in Vancouver and some really great museums.

2 **Read the sentences and say which person they refer to.**

1 Who stayed in a place where the water is freezing?
2 Who went to Nevada?
3 Who saw strange rocks and trees?
4 Who stayed in a cold house?
5 Who will go to Mexico this year?
6 Who will go somewhere colder this year?

Listening

27 **3** **Listen and draw the correct weather symbols on the map.**

Key

 sunny

 rainy / showers

 cloudy

 snowy

 foggy

 stormy/ thunderstorms

 windy

Speaking

4 **Work with a partner and discuss today's weather. What do you think it will be like tomorrow?**

A Today, the weather is…

B What will it be like tomorrow?

A I think it will be…

Speaking

5 **Complete the quiz about your future. Then discuss your answers with a partner.**

When I am older, I think I will ...

	Yes	No		Yes	No
• go to college	☐	☐	• run a business	☐	☐
• live in another country	☐	☐	• be rich	☐	☐
• stay in the same place	☐	☐	• get married	☐	☐
• live near my family	☐	☐	• drive a sports car	☐	☐
• be an English teacher	☐	☐	• be famous	☐	☐

A Will you go to college in the future?

B Yes, I will. / No, I won't. What about you?

Writing for your Portfolio

6 **Read about Sarah's future and then write about yourself.**

My future

I think I might be a famous explorer when I'm older because I like seeing different places and meeting people. I won't be very rich because I'll travel all the time. I'll live in the same country as I live now, near my family and friends, and I'll have a nice sports car and a beautiful house. What about you?

Aurora Borealis—the Northern Lights

Key words

cosmic weather	North / South Pole	moon	oxygen
high temperature	solar / lunar eclipse	phenomenon	nitrogen
particles	lightning	electric fields	oval-shaped
magnetic field	meteor	gas	

1 **Read the texts.**

The photos on this page show a "natural laser show" known as the Northern Lights. You can see this light show in many different countries in the world, including the northern United States and Canada. The Northern Lights are clearest during winter nights. During these nights, the sky often turns red, green, blue, or violet. Although we cannot always see them, the auroras are always there. They cover the North and South Pole and are oval-shaped.

The Finnish name for the Northern lights is *revontulet*, which means "fox fires." The name comes from an old story. It says that the arctic fox throws up snow with its big bushy tail. The snow goes high up into the sky and starts a fire, the "fox fire."

Some Inuit people, a native group in Alaska, were once scared of the Northern Lights. They thought they were very dangerous, especially for children. They told their children not to go outside when they were in the sky. They thought the Northern Lights would kill the children!

Where do the Northern Lights really come from?

Science

2a **Read the text.**

What causes the different colors?

Auroras are always two colors–blue and red or green and red. The colors of the aurora depend on which different gases are in the atmosphere. Nitrogen causes the red and blue lights and oxygen causes the red and green lights. There is more nitrogen gas in the atmosphere nearest to Earth's surface. That is why the sky sometimes looks very red, almost like it's on fire.

2b **Look at the pictures of the Northern Lights on page 112. Decide if the main gas is nitrogen or oxygen.**

Mini-project

3 **Complete the explanations for four other phenomena by using one of the words below to fill in the blank.**

rainbow	sun	lightning	moon

1 When there is a solar eclipse, the moon goes in front of the …….. .

2 When there is a lunar eclipse, Earth is between the .... and the sun. Earth's shadow falls on the moon so we cannot see it.

3 A ……….. happens when it is raining and the light of the sun shines on the raindrops.

4 …………… happens when ice crystals and water drops in the air bump together to cause electricity.

4 **Choose one of the phenomena in Exercise 3. In small groups, draw a diagram to show how the phenomenon works. Use the Internet or a library to help you.**

UNIT 12

What if ...?

In this unit

You learn

- *If* clauses
- possessive pronouns
- questions with *Whose?*
- words for vacations

and then you can

- talk about alternatives
- suggestions and preferences

28 **1 Listen and read.**

Mom Look. It says here if we book early, we'll get 10 percent off.

Sally What for?

Mom A vacation in a cabin on Lake Erie.

Harry I don't want to go there. There isn't enough to do. If you go there, I'll go and stay with Grandpa and Grandma.

Sally Well if he stays, I'll stay too. I'll go and stay with Lisa.

Dad No way! You're both coming with us.

Harry Staying with Lisa? Was that your idea or hers?

Sally Actually, it wasn't hers or mine. It was her parents' idea. They asked me last week.

Dad Well, I want us to take a vacation together as a family. What about taking a road trip to Aunt Maria's?

Sally Not again! It's way too far to drive.

Mom Well, why don't we go somewhere different, like Alaska? I've always wanted to go to Alaska.

Harry If we go there, I'll freeze. I can't stand cold weather.

Dad If we can't agree on something, we'll just have to stay home.

Harry Great! Then we can spend our summer vacation discussing next year's vacation!

2 **Complete the sentences.**

1 If they book early, they'll get…
2 Harry doesn't want to go to Lake Erie because…
3 Sally wants to stay…
4 Dad wants to go…
5 Mom has always wanted to…
6 Harry doesn't want to go to Alaska because…

Sounds right /i/ /ɪ/

29 **3** **Listen. Circle the /i/ sounds and underline the /ɪ/ sounds.**

freeze is we'll swim sea if beach him it

30 **4** **Now listen and repeat.**

We'll swim in the sea if it doesn't freeze.

Get talking Talking about alternatives

31 **5** **Listen and repeat.**

Girl Let's go to the beach.
Boy But what if it rains?
Girl Then we'll watch TV at your place.
Boy OK.

Boy Let's go swimming.
Girl But what if it's too cold?
Boy Then we won't stay in too long.

6 **Work with a partner. Match the phrases from columns A, B, and C to make dialogues similar to those in Exercise 5.**

	A		B		C
Let's…	• take the bus. • go to the movie theater. • use the computer. • go to Chile on vacation.	But what if…	• the bus is late. • the computer doesn't work. • it's too hot. • there are no more tickets.	Then	• we'll go and see another movie. • we'll write the letter. • we'll take sunscreen and hats. • we'll take a taxi.

Language Focus

Vocabulary Vacations

1 Write the correct numbers of the phrases in the pictures.

1 take a vacation
2 go sightseeing
3 buy souvenirs
4 go camping
5 stay in a hotel
6 take photographs
7 go hiking
8 stay with relatives
9 go to the beach
10 send postcards

Get talking Suggestions and preferences

32 **2 Listen and repeat.**

A Let's go to Hawaii on vacation.
B Hawaii? No, I'd rather go to Mexico.

A Let's go camping this year.
B Camping? No, I'd rather go hiking.

3 Work with a partner. Make conversations like the ones in Exercise 2. Use the ideas in the boxes.

go to Seattle / go to New York City	stay in a hotel / stay with friends
stay in a hotel / go camping	go to the beach / go hiking
take photographs / write postcards	go sightseeing / buy souvenirs

Grammar

If clauses

1 **Put the words in order to make the examples. Check against the dialogue on page 114.**

we'll / we / book / If / get / early, / discount / 10 percent.
go / If / there, / freeze. / we / I'll

To make a first conditional sentence, use the structure below:
If + subject + simple present / subject + **will/won't** + verb

If **you write** to her, **she'll be** very happy.
If **it's cold, we won't go** out.

If **you don't write** to her, **she'll be** unhappy.
If **it isn't** cold, **we'll go** out.

2 **Complete the sentences with the correct form of the verb.**

1 If we win the money, we .... (buy) a new house.
2 We .... (go) on vacation if there is time.
3 If we .... (need) some help, we'll ask.
4 She .... (not write) to you if she leaves.
5 If Harry stays with his grandparents, Sally .... (not be) happy.
6 We .... (do) this for you if you want.

3 **Circle the correct form to complete the sentences.**

1 If we *will win / win* the final, my team *will be / are* the best.
2 If you *do / don't do* what your teacher says, you *'ll be / be* in trouble.
3 If the phone *works / doesn't work*, we *return / 'll return* it to the store.
4 If you *will be / are* late, we *go / 'll go* to the movie theater without you.
5 If my parents *come back / will come back* from vacation, we *won't / will* have the party.
6 They *will buy / won't buy* the computer if it *will cost / costs* too much.
7 If he *is / will be* tired, he *will / won't* come.

4 **Complete the dialogue using the phrases below.**

it rains
our parents say no
's no party

A Let's have an end-of-summer party on the beach on Friday.
B Good idea. But what if [1]...................................... ?
C We can have the party at my place.
A Ok. But what if [2].......................... ?
D Then there [3].. !

5 **Work with a partner. Student A chooses one of the suggestions below. Student B thinks of *But what if...* answers. Student A makes an alternative suggestion. Switch roles.**

A We could take a bike ride next Sunday.
B Great idea. But what if it rains?
A We'll go the weekend after next!

Let's take a vacation to Arizona this year.

Let's write a school magazine in English and sell it to our parents.

Let's organize a football game against the teachers in our school.

We could go swimming on Saturday.

Possessive pronouns

6 **Look at the dialogue on page 114 and complete the examples.**

Was that your idea or [1]................?
Actually it wasn't [2]................ or [3]................

my – **mine**	his – **his**	our – **ours**
your – **yours**	her – **hers**	your – **yours**
	its – **its**	their – **theirs**

We use possessive pronouns to say who something belongs to. We use them instead of a noun.
Was that your idea or **hers**? (= Was that your idea or **her idea**?)
It wasn't **hers** or **mine**. (= It wasn't **her idea** or **my idea**.)
I found this pen. Is it **yours**? (= Is it **your pen**?)
No, it's **his**. (= No, it's **his pen**.)

Questions with *Whose ...?*

Use ***Whose...?*** to ask who something belongs to.
"**Whose** coat is this?" "It's Jane's" or "It's **hers**."

7 **Write questions with *Whose...?* and answers using possessive pronouns.**

1 this diary? – Tim's diary
A Whose diary is this.................................?
B It's his...

2 these books? – Maria's books
....?
....

3 that camera? – my camera
....?
....

4 those black T-shirts – Mark and Harry's T-shirts
....?
....

5 these green sneakers – your sneakers
....?
....

Reading

1 **How much do you remember about your English book? Take the quiz to find out.**

Book Quiz

1  Abigail and Steve watched a scary DVD in Unit 2. What was its name?

a ☐ *The Window*
b ☐ *The Door*
c ☐ *The Garden*

2 In Unit 3, Mark went on a trip and saw this. Where did he go?

a ☐ Mexico
b ☐ Indonesia
c ☐ Guatemala

3 In Unit 4 you met this fantastic animal from Atlantis. What was it called?

a ☐ a Snapkle
b ☐ a Ruckle
c ☐ a Hipcop

4 In Unit 5 Sally and Simon go on strike. Why? For:

a ☐ more money
b ☐ no more homework
c ☐ no housework

5 This is Brittany from Unit 6. Which school did she go to?

a ☐ Dance school
b ☐ Drama school
c ☐ Primary school

6 In Unit 7, Sally and Harry are going to visit this place. What is it called?

a ☐ Six Flags
b ☐ The Odeon
c ☐ All Fun Park

7 What did Fido want in Unit 8?

a ☐ chicken soup
b ☐ a bone
c ☐ steak and chips

8 In Unit 9 we met these people. What is the name of their planet?

a ☐ Trojan
b ☐ Juno
c ☐ Jupiter

9 In Unit 10, Sally, Harry, and Olivia are trying to find a place. Which place?

a ☐ the mall
b ☐ the post office
c ☐ the movie theater

10 In Unit 11, this student had a science test. What was his name?

a ☐ Walter the Worrier
b ☐ William the Worrier
c ☐ William the Worker

Score / 10

Listening

33 **2** **Listen and check your answers. Score 1 point for every answer you get right.**

A Song 4 U We are on vacation

34 **3** **Listen and complete the song using the words on the left. Then sing along!**

classes
teachers
Maine
watch
rings
meet
plans
end
pack
beach

When the school bell 1.......................,
at a quarter to four,
and we 2....................... up our things,
and we walk out that door.
And we say goodbye,
to the 3....................... and friends,
it's the end of June
and school's at an 4....................... .

Chorus
We can do anything, we can go anywhere.
No more 5....................... for a long, long time.
We are on vacation, our summer vacation.
We're on vacation, we feel fine, we feel fine.

Do you have any 6.......................
about what you do with your time?
Let's go to the 7.......................
if the weather is fine.

Are you going away
to the Carolinas or 8....................... ?
Or are you going to stay
at home and play?

Chorus

If you feel bored,
just give me a call.
We can 9....................... up
at the mall.
Or see a movie
On DVD,
or instead we can
10....................... TV.

We can do anything, we can go anywhere.
We are on vacation, our vacation.

Chorus (x 2)

Writing for your Portfolio

4 **Read Peter's plans for his next vacation. Then write about yourself.**

My next vacation
My next vacation is in July. I'm not sure what I'm going to do. We often go to Florida and stay with my aunt and uncle. If my parents go there, I'll go with them. But if we stay at home, I'll hang out with my friends and play video games and watch DVDs and things like that.
I want to go to Florida because it's a lot of fun. The weather is always nice and there are a lot of things to do.

MORE fun with Fido

Check your progress Units 11 and 12

1 Write the weather words.

 ....

 ....

 ....

 ....

 5 ....

 6 ....

 7 ....

7

2 Complete with *will, won't,* or *might*.

A I think it [1].................... rain tomorrow.
B I don't think so. I think it [2]....................
be sunny. It [3].................... be cloudy but it
definitely [4].................... be rainy.
A I think I [5].................... go to the beach.
B I [6].................... come with you or I
[7].................... stay at home.
A [8].................... you come shopping with me now?
B OK!

8

3 Complete the sentences with the correct possessive pronouns.

1 This is Mark's book. It's ....
2 That was Mark and Sally's house. It was ....
3 This is my computer. It's ....
4 That was Sally's money. It was ....
5 This is your pen. It's ....

5

4 Complete the first conditional sentences.

1 If we stay at home, we .... (miss) the show.
2 We .... (ask) about it, if you want.
3 If he .... (want) it, we'll buy it.
4 If it .... (not / work), we'll return it.
5 They .... (not / go) on vacation this year if their friends come to see them.

10

5 Complete the dialogue. Use the first conditional.

A [1]..?
(you come to the concert / I buy the ticket)
B Yes, I [2]....................
A I [3].................... (ask) Jack if he [4]....................
(want) to come too. And Frankie.
B If Frankie [5].................... (come), I
[6].................... definitely go!
A OK. If I [7].................... (see) her, I [8]....................
(ask) her.
B If she [9].................... (not want) to come, I
[10].................... (ask) her out somewhere else.
A You must really like her!

10

6 Write the questions.

1 ....?
It's rainy and windy in Chicago.
2 ....?
No, they won't be here tomorrow.
3 ....?
Yes, he will pay for it.
4 ....?
No, it won't rain next week.
5 ....?
It's his car.

10

TOTAL 50

My progress so far is ...

- great! ☐
- good. ☐
- poor. ☐

Learn MORE about Culture

Extreme weather

1 **Which photograph shows a hurricane and which a tornado?**

1 HURRICANES – THE FACTS –

* Hurricanes come from the ocean.
* They travel at more than 100 km per hour.
* They can be from 100 to 1,600 km wide.
* Hurricanes are given names, for example, Hurricane Andrew.

A) ______

B) ______

2 TORNADOES – THE FACTS –

* There are about 800 to 1,200 tornadoes a year in the U.S.
* They are usually in Northwest Texas, Oklahoma, and Kansas.
* They circle around at speeds of 320 to 800 km per hour.
* They are a dark gray color because they pick up soil and other objects.

2 **Read Jimmy's story and answer the questions.**

1 When did Hurricane Katrina hit New Orleans?
2 Where was Jimmy when the hurricane happened?
3 How high did the water rise?
4 How fast was the wind?
5 How long did Jimmy wait to be rescued?

Jimmy's Story

In 2005, Hurricane Katrina hit New Orleans, and Jimmy Lewis's world fell apart. Jimmy stayed home, thinking that he would be able to make it through the hurricane. On Sunday night, the wind blew at 200km/hour. But Jimmy didn't worry—until water began to flood into his house. It filled up the first floor, then it filled up the second. Jimmy went into the attic. After a two-day wait, Jimmy was rescued. Now he feels lucky to be alive.

35 **3** **Listen and circle T (True) or F (False).**

The Storm Chasers!
Most people run away or hide from hurricanes and tornadoes, but some people in the U.S. actually chase them! You can even take a storm-chasing vacation!

1 Storm-chasing tours are not safe. T / F
2 If you go on the tour, you will have breakfast at 8:00 a.m. T / F
3 The tornadoes are always far from the hotel. T / F
4 You can't take photos of the tornadoes. T / F
5 If there aren't any tornadoes, they go sightseeing. T / F

4 **Over 2 U!** **Write about a weather disaster in your country.**

MORE! Now you can watch Episode 6 of *Kids in NYC!* DVD

strange weather stories

1 The day the sun rained

Once when I was a boy, I was playing football in the back yard of our house. It was a beautiful sunny day, but suddenly I saw some big black clouds in the sky. They were coming our way. I went to the front of the house to tell my mother, because the laundry was drying on the clothesline in the back yard. When I got to the front door, it was already raining heavily. My mother and I went to the back yard again, but when we got there, there was nothing but sun. It was very strange! When we looked one way, there was rain. When we looked the other way, there was sun. We call it "the day the sun rained."

2 Above the clouds

About five years ago, I was on vacation in New York City. It was really hot. The temperature was over 40°C. My friend and I decided to go to the top of the Empire State Building. "The air will be cooler up there," we thought. We were wrong, and it was very hot at the top, too. There were some clouds coming toward us and suddenly a thunderstorm started, but because we were so high up, the storm was below us. We looked down and saw the lightning and the rain falling, but we didn't get wet. It was so weird!

3 Raining frogs

I've got a really strange story about the weather. It's true, I promise, but not many people believe me. One day, when I was about 10, I was fishing with my brother when I saw a small frog hopping in the grass next to me. That wasn't strange. I was next to a river. But then I saw a splash in the water and another frog, and then another. I looked at my brother and he looked at me. We looked at the sky. There were some clouds but it wasn't raining. It was really strange. I looked at the ground. There were now about five frogs hopping about. Then I felt something hit me on my head. I put my hand on it and—yuck—there was a frog on top of me. It jumped off and then jumped away. After that we didn't see any more frogs or splashes. It sounds weird but I know that what we saw was frog rain.

For MORE! Go to www.more-online.com/american and take a quiz on this text.

Herbert Puchta & Jeff Stranks
G. Gerngross C. Holzmann P. Lewis-Jones

American MORE! 2B

COMBO Workbook

HELBLING LANGUAGES
CAMBRIDGE UNIVERSITY PRESS
editora ática

CONTENTS

UNIT 7 On the weekend

1 Reorder the phrases to make a dialogue.

Dialogue 1

- [ ] **Christina** I'm spending the evening at school.
- [ ] **Michelle** Really? Till midnight?
- [ ] **Christina** Yeah, we're having a video evening with our language teachers.
- [ ] **Michelle** At school?
- [ ] **Christina** Yeah, till midnight.
- [ ] **Michelle** Cool. Can I come too?
- [1] **Michelle** What are you doing tomorrow evening, Christina?

Dialogue 2

- [ ] **Oliver** OK. See you Monday!
- [1] **Tim** What are you doing this weekend?
- [ ] **Oliver** Oh, they're fun! There are a lot of great rides.
- [ ] **Tim** No, thanks. I don't really like theme parks.
- [ ] **Oliver** I'm going to Luna Park with some friends. Would you like to come?
- [ ] **Tim** Anyway, I'm going to the mall on Saturday, and I'm going to a football game on Sunday.

Making suggestions

2 Write short dialogues using the expressions below.

Let's… How about…? Why don't we…? We could… Should we…?

A What are we doing tomorrow?
B ....
A That's a great idea!

A ....
B ....
A ....

A ....
B ....
A ....

A ....
B ....
A ....

Language Focus

Vocabulary Sports

1 Write the name of each sport.

1 ....

2 ....

3 ....

4 ....

5 ....

6 ....

2 Reorder the letters and write the name of the sport.

1 ninurgn ....
2 sinnte ....
3 etallbbask ....
4 lofabotl ....
5 msiigwmn ....
6 satengkodbrai ....

Talking about sports

3 Complete the dialogue with the words below.

tennis twice favorite game often sport

Nicole What's your [1] .... sport, Matthew?
Matthew Hmm, probably basketball. But I also like [2] ....
Nicole Are you a good tennis player?
Matthew I'm OK, I think.
Nicole How [3] .... do you play?
Matthew What? Tennis or basketball?
Nicole Both.
Matthew Well, I play tennis [4] .... a week and basketball four times a week. I'm on a baseketball team.
Nicole Oh really? You play a lot of sports!
Matthew True. What about you? What's your favorite [5] .... ?
Nicole Watching basketball on TV.
Matthew Well, do you want to watch tomorrow's [6] .... with me?
Nicole Sure, why not.

4 Match the questions and answers.

1 What's your favorite sport?
2 Who's your favorite athlete.
3 How often do you go swimming?
4 What's your favorite football team?
5 Do you like volleyball?

a No, not really.
b Three or four times a week.
c She's a skier, but I can't think of her name right now.
d The New York Giants.
e Running.

Grammar

Time prepositions *on, at, in*

1 Write *on*, *at*, or *in*.

It happened [1] .... Friday last week. It was [2] .... a sunny day [3] .... spring. I woke up in my hotel room [4] .... six o'clock [5] .... the morning. I went downstairs to have some breakfast, but there was nobody there. Usually there were three or four people [6] .... breakfast early [7] .... the morning. I went back upstairs and came down again [8] .... nine o'clock. Still nobody. Then I came down again [9] .... noon. There was no one in the hotel. Something had happened during the night. Then I woke up!

2 Match the halves of each sentence.

1 We're leaving for
2 Are you cleaning your
3 Jenny's coming to
4 Martin is going
5 I'm doing my

a homework this afternoon, but then I'm free.
b room this evening?
c to the movie with Tom tomorrow evening.
d my party on Saturday!
e Cancún next Sunday.

Present continuous Future

3 Read the diary and write what Sara is doing each evening.

Monday	go to volleyball practice
Tuesday	work on a biology project for school with Tom
Wednesday	take a writing class
Thursday	buy Tom's present
Friday	meet Monica!
Saturday	go to Tom's party!

On Monday evening, she's going to volleyball practice.
....
....
....
....
....

4 **Rewrite the sentences in the negative form.**

1 They are arriving in Chicago on Monday. ....
2 He is finishing work tomorrow. ....
3 She is spending spring break at home. ....
4 I'm leaving for Florida tomorrow. ....
5 We are going out tonight. ....

5 **Write the questions and short answers.**

1 you / are / dinner / to / coming – no Are you coming to dinner? No, I'm not.
2 playing / the / are / next / you / game / in – no ....
3 they / today / driving / to / the lake / are – yes ....
4 going / evening / to / is / theater / she / the / tomorrow – yes ....
5 at / they / home / evening / this / are / eating – no ....

6 **Match the questions and answers.**

1 What are you doing on Sunday?
2 Are you helping John tomorrow?
3 What's Sarah doing tomorrow?
4 Where's John meeting us?
5 Who isn't coming to the party tomorrow?
6 Are you playing football next Monday?

a Jenny. She's visiting her aunt.
b At the mall, I think.
c No, we aren't playing any more games this month.
d No, certainly not. He never helps me!
e I'm working until lunchtime.
f She's playing in a basketball tournament.

7a **Write questions to ask people you know.**

1 What / do / this evening? ....?
2 What / have / for dinner this evening? ....?
3 Where / go / on vacation this year? ....?
4 How / go / to school tomorrow? ....?
5 What / do / on the weekend? ....?

7b **Ask the questions in Exercise 7a. Write the name of the person and his or her answer below.**

Name	**Answer**

Grammar for Communication

19 **Complete the dialogue with the verbs below. Then listen and check.**

helping watching doing writing going

1 **Martin** What are you doing on Saturday, Susan?
Susan Not much. I'm [1] .... some old DVDs.
Martin Aren't you going to the movies?
Susan No, there's nothing new on. What are you doing?
Martin I'm [2] .... to the mall with some friends.
Susan Sounds good. Can I come?
Martin Sure! Good idea!

2 **Phil** What are you [3] .... this evening?
Laura I'm [4] .... my essay for English.
Phil Really?
Laura Why don't you do yours, too? We could help each other.
Phil I'm sorry, I can't. I'm [5] .... my dad with his new computer.

Skills

Reading

1a **Read the texts.**

What do you usually do on Saturdays?

1 I always get up early on Saturdays to go shopping with my dad. We go to a grocery store and shop for the whole week. Then he takes me to the mall and we go to the music stores. I like looking for new music, but my dad likes jazz. I'm a hip-hop fan. The two of us always spend hours in the music stores. After lunch, I do some homework or spend an hour or two in front of my computer and listen to some music on my MP3 player. Then I usually meet my friends. We go to the park or the mall and talk about music and football and play games.

2 I usually get up early on the weekend. I live in the country and there is a lot to do here. My grandma and some uncles and aunts live close to us. I like it here. We have a huge yard. I like to play tennis or go for walks with my two dogs.

On Saturdays when the weather is bad, I get up late. I might do a little homework and sometimes I like to watch sports on TV. I'm a big football fan, and some of my best friends are football fans, too. We like to go and see games, too.

1b **Write the name of the person who says these things.**

1 My father is a jazz fan. ....
2 I usually get up early. ....
3 I live in the country. ....
4 We meet at the park or the mall. ....
5 I like to play tennis. ....

Skills

Listening

20 **2** **Listen and decide if the sentences are T (True) or F (False).**

1 On Saturday morning, Janet is going shopping with her friend. T / F
2 They are shopping for clothes. T / F
3 The concert starts at 8:00 p.m. T / F
4 Doug is also going to the concert. T / F
5 One of Janet's cousins is going to the concert, too. T / F
6 Doug's dad is picking them up after the concert. T / F
7 On Sunday, Doug and his friends are working on a biology project. T / F
8 Janet is meeting Kathy on Sunday. T / F
9 They are doing homework together. T / F

Speaking

3 **Use the pictures that describe Henry's weekend and complete the dialogue.**

	Saturday	Sunday
mornings		
afternoons		
evenings		

A What does Henry usually do on Saturday mornings?
B He usually [1] ....
A Where does he usually go on Saturday afternoons?
B [2] ....
A Does he usually go out on Sunday evenings?
B [3] ....
A Does he usually sleep in on Sunday mornings?
B [4] ....
A When does he usually go out?
B [5] ....
A When does he usually do his homework?
B [6] ....

Writing for your Portfolio

4 **Rewrite the dialogue from Exercise 3 about yourself. Remember to change the subject, verb, and pronouns. Start like this:**

A *What do you do on Saturday mornings?*
Me ....
A ....
Me ....
A ....
Me ....
A ....
Me ....
A ....
Me ....
A ....
Me ....

UNIT 8 It hurts!

1 Complete the dialogue with the words below.

headache wasn't test math was evening

Dad Sarah has a terrible [1] .... today. She's staying in bed.

Mark No, she doesn't! She doesn't want to go to school today! She has a [2] .... test today.

Dad A math test? Really? She [3] .... studying very much last night. She [4] .... watching TV with me in the living room.

Mark Exactly! I have a [5] .... today but I was studying last night. I wasn't watching TV all [6] ....

Sarah Oh be quiet, Mark! I'll go to school!

Saying what someone was doing

2 Look at the pictures and answer the questions.

1 What was Alan doing at 11:00 a.m.?

....

2 What was Emma doing at 8:00 p.m.?

....

3 What was Mike doing at 10:00 a.m.?

....

4 What was Sue doing at 10:00 a.m.?

....

5 What was Dave doing at 6:30 p.m.?

....

6 What was Mel doing at 5:45 p.m.?

....

3 Write a question for each answer. Use the words in parentheses below and the pictures from Exercise 2.

1 No, he was reading a comic book. (read a newspaper) *Was Alan reading a newspaper?*
2 No, she was watching TV. (listen to music) ....
3 No, he was running in the park. (buy a present) ....
4 No, she was walking her dog. (play basketball) ....
5 No, he was on the computer. (meet friends) ....
6 No, she was washing the dishes. (sleep on the beach) ....

Language Focus

Vocabulary Aches and pains

1 **Look at the picture and complete the sentences with a word from below:**

toothache backache headache stomachache
earache cold sore throat knee hurts

1 Tom has an earache
2 Mr. Smith has a ....
3 Sally has a ....
4 Mrs. Davis has a ....
5 Stefan has a ....
6 Jill has a ....
7 Mr. Anwar has a ....
8 Mrs. Heals's ....

Talking about sickness

2 **Reorder the words in each line and write a dialogue between a doctor and his patients.**

1 **Doctor** Smith / the matter with / What's / you / Mr.
What's the matter with you Mr Smith?

Mr. Smith a terrible / stomach / my / I have / in / pain
....

2 **Doctor** too / your / Does / hurt, / leg?
....

Mrs. Heals knee / it's / No, / my / just
....

3 **Doctor** OK / you / Are / Jill?
....

Jill feeling / No, / dizzy / a little / I'm
....

Grammar

Past continuous Affirmative and negative

1 Circle the correct form of the verb.

1 Paul *was / were* playing volleyball at 3:00 p.m.
2 My dad *was / were* driving his car to work at 8:00 a.m.
3 The children *was / were* watching TV all afternoon.
4 The dog *wasn't / weren't* eating a bone, he *was / were* eating your dinner!
5 I *wasn't / weren't* doing my homework at 11:00 p.m. I was in bed.
6 They *was / were* sitting on the sofa but they *wasn't / weren't* watching TV.

2 Look at the pictures and complete the sentences.

1 Dad was reading the newspaper at eight o'clock.

2 Fred and Jill ....

3 Mom ....

4 The baby ....

5 Alan and Jason ....

6 Jane ....

Past continuous Questions and short answers

3 Look at the pictures in Exercise 2 again and answer the questions.

1 Was Dad reading a book at eight o'clock?
No, he wasn't. He was reading a newspaper.
2 Were Fred and Jill playing tennis at noon?
....
3 Was the baby sleeping at five o'clock?
....
4 Were Alan and Jason playing football at 11 o'clock? ....

4 Write questions and answer them about yourself.

1 eat breakfast / 7:00 a.m.
Were you eating breakfast at 7:00 a.m.? Yes, I was. / No, I wasn't. I was sleeping.
2 study math / 11:00 a.m. yesterday
....
3 talk on the telephone / 6:00 p.m. yesterday
....

Superlatives

5 Complete the table.

adjective	superlative	adjective	superlative
long	1 *the longest*	beautiful	5
big	2	dangerous	6
small	3	good	7
ugly	4	bad	8

6 Look at the table from Exercise 5 and complete the sentences with an adjective or the superlative.

1 What a ...*long*...... day. I'm happy it's over.
2 They live in a .... house in the town. It has 15 bedrooms.
3 We have five dogs. Benny is .... He's tiny!!
4 He's not ...., but he's not very handsome either.
5 I think Beyoncé is .... woman in the world.
6 Don't go near that dog. He's .... dog on this street.
7 Danni did great. She got .... grade!
8 Don't go and see it. It's .... movie ever!

7 Complete the sentences with the superlative.

1 Charles and George are good at math, but Bob is ....*the best*....
2 Monday and Tuesday were cold, but Wednesday was ....
3 Your bag is heavy. His bag is heavier, but my bag is ....
4 Her sisters are beautiful, but Mary is ....
5 Dave and Trevor are both hungry, but Johnny is ....

8 Harry, Larry, and Barry are triplets. Look at the picture. Use the adjectives below and write sentences.

~~tall~~ old heavy smart short young handsome

	Harry	Barry	Larry
born	02/02/94 10:02 a.m.	02/02/94 10:50 a.m.	02/02/94 11:40 a.m.
last school grades	All Cs	All Bs	All As
weight	70kg	63kg	73kg

1 *Harry is the tallest.*
2 ....
3 ....
4 ....
5 ....
6 ....
7 ....

Grammar for Communication

21 **Complete the dialogue with the sentences below. Then listen and check.**

I was at Sue Brown's house. We were watching DVDs.
No, you weren't. I was at my friend's house.

Mark What were you doing last night?
Emma [1] ....
Mark Which friend was that?
Emma Sue. I was at her house all evening.
Mark [2] ....
I was at Sue's house at 8:00 p.m. and you weren't there.
Emma Yes, I was. [3] ....
Mark Were you at Sue Mather's house?
Emma No, [4] ....
Mark Oh! I see!!

Skills

Listening

22 **1 Listen to the story of "The Pink Pill" and number the pictures in the correct order.**

2 Read the sentences and decide if they are True, False, or Doesn't say.

	True	False	Doesn't say
1 The doctor's name is Dr. James.	☐	☐	☐
2 The man's name is Mr. Wilkins.	☐	☐	☐
3 The doctor gives him a yellow pill for his headache.	☐	☐	☐
4 The man's wife told him about the pink pill.	☐	☐	☐
5 He gets a green pill on Wednesday.	☐	☐	☐
6 On Thursday, the man has three health problems.	☐	☐	☐
7 The man finally gets the pink pill on Thursday.	☐	☐	☐
8 The man riding the bike was his friend.	☐	☐	☐

Skills

Reading

3 Read Sally's letter to the students in her class and answer the questions.

Hi Everyone,

Thanks for the Get Well Soon card and letter. It was great to hear all your news. I laughed a lot when I was reading it. I'm quite enjoying my time at home. Sometimes it's great! Yesterday, for example, I played computer games, watched three movies on DVD, read a cool comic book, and sent a lot of text messages. That was fun. But sometimes I get a little bored too, so if you have some free time, come and visit me, please!

I was thinking of everyone at 3:00 p.m. on Saturday. We were playing the big game against East High. I already know that we won and that Fred scored a touchdown. That's amazing! Congratulations to everyone.

The doctor says I can come back at the end of next week, but I can't play soccer or any other sports until May.

See you all soon, Sally.

1 Why did Sally like the letter from her class? ....

2 What did she do yesterday? ....

3 Why does she invite them to visit her? ....

4 What was she doing at 3:00 p.m. on Saturday? ....

5 Who won the football game? ....

6 When can she go back to school? ....

Writing for your Portfolio

4 Imagine you have broken an arm or a leg and you can't go to school for two weeks. The other students in your class write you a letter hoping you get well soon. Answer it. Use the letter from Exercise 3 as a model.

....

....

....

....

....

....

....

....

....

....

....

UNIT 9 Guess what?

1 **Complete the dialogue using the phrases below.**

as I went toward | was walking home | they were playing | what happened | they were moving

Mike Guess [1] .... to me yesterday?

Sarah What?

Mike Well, I [2] .... last night and I saw all these bright lights in the sky. [3] .... and changing color.

Sarah How strange!

Mike And there were noises.

Sarah Wow. What do you think it was?

Mike Well, [4] .... the lights, I realized it was the opening of a new restaurant in town. It has lights on the roof and [5] .... some great music!

Giving reasons

2 **Look at the pictures and write sentences using *because* and the expressions below.**

~~happy~~	~~called~~
scared	watch a horror movie
go to the dentist's	have a toothache
crash into a tree	drive too fast
have a shower	play soccer
stay in bed	have a cold

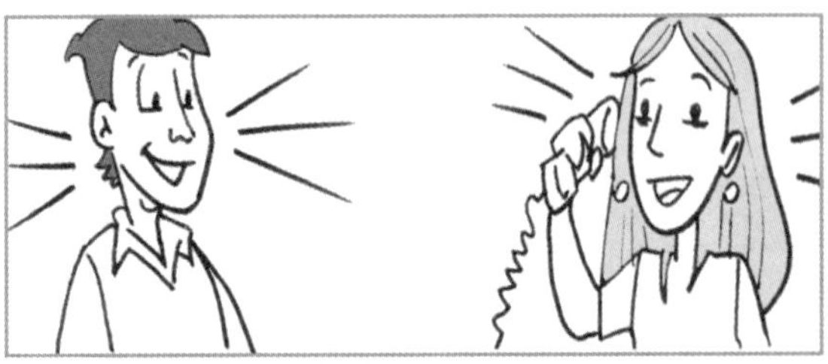

1 I was happy because Janice called me.

2 ....

3 ....

4 ....

5 ....

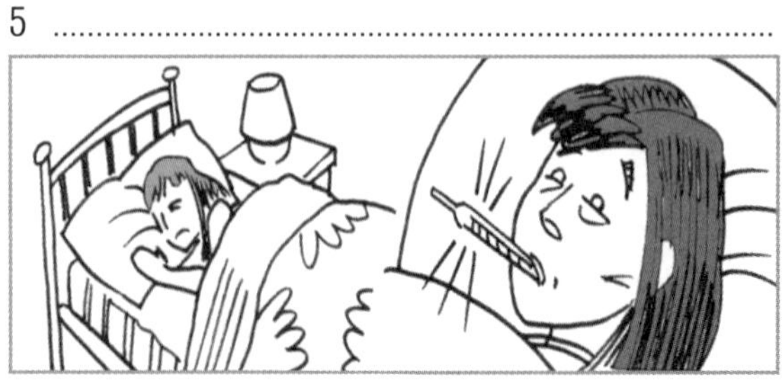

6 ....

Language Focus

Vocabulary Emotions

1 Reorder the letters and write words to describe the emotions below.

1 frightened........ 2 .... 3 .... 4 .... 5 ....

6 .... 7 .... 8 .... 9 .... 10 ....

Talking about emotions

2 Complete the sentences with words from Exercise 1.

1 If you feel frightened........, think of something else!
2 If you feel ...., find something to do!
3 If you feel ...., cry!
4 If you feel ...., count to 10!
5 If you feel ...., smile!
6 If you feel ...., talk to a friend!

3 Answer the questions.
How do you feel when ...

1	it's your birthday?	I feel happy when it's my birthday.
2	you lose some money?	
3	you fail a test?	
4	you watch a horror movie?	
5	your football team loses?	
6	it rains all weekend?	
7	the summer starts?	
8	the teacher asks you a difficult question?	

Grammar

Past continuous vs. simple past

1 Circle the expression that shows the shortest action in the sentences below.

1 I was watching TV when the phone rang.
2 We were playing tennis when I broke my racket.
3 When the ball broke the window, we were eating breakfast.
4 When the lights went out, I was working at the computer.
5 She was dancing when she fell.
6 The children were playing in the yard when the dog escaped.

2 Circle the correct verb below.

1 I can't do my homework because I *was* / *wasn't* listening when the teacher explained it.
2 She's not wearing a hat because it *was* / *wasn't* raining when she left home.
3 We're tired because we *were* / *weren't* working all evening.
4 I didn't answer the phone because I *was* / *wasn't* watching a movie on TV.
5 He doesn't know what happened because he *was* / *wasn't* there.

3 Write sentences using the pictures and the words.

1 Emma broke leg / play soccer

Emma broke her leg when
she was playing soccer.

2 start raining / Sarah walk dog

....

....

3 chair break / Tom work at the computer

....

....

4 her headache start / Sue read a book

....

....

5 crash into a tree / Paul listen to his MP3 player

....

....

6 Karen fall asleep / teacher talk

....

....

one / ones

4 Circle *one* or *ones* in the sentences below.

1 **A** I'd like to try some glasses on?
B Which *one / ones*—the red or the blue?

2 **A** Have you seen this movie?
B Yes, it's the *one / ones* with Tom Cruise and Penelope Cruz.

3 **A** Would you like an ice cream cone?
B No, I don't want *one / ones*, but thanks.

4 **A** How much are those shirts?
B This *one / ones* is $35.

5 **A** I like those earrings.
B I prefer the *one / ones* with the blue stones.

6 **A** I'm getting a new computer next week.
B Make sure you get *one / ones* with a DVD writer.

Quantity *a lot of / much / many*

5a Circle the noncount nouns.

students rabbits money water days sugar noise light

5b Now, circle the correct expression of quantity.

1 *A lot of / Not much / Not many* rabbits.

2 *A lot of / Not much / Not many* money.

3 *A lot of / Not much / Not many* sugar.

4 *A lot of / Not much / Not many* days until the New Year!

5 *A lot of / Not much / Not many* light.

6 *A lot of / Not much / Not many* noise.

7 *A lot of / Not much / Not many* students.

8 *A lot of / Not much / Not many* water.

6 Complete with *much or many*.

1 There isn't ...much... money left.
2 There's not .... time now. Hurry!
3 There are not .... good restaurants in this town. It's hard to get a good meal.
4 She has .... friends. She is very popular.
5 There are not .... people as intelligent as her. She's a genius.

Grammar for Communication

23 **Complete the dialogue with the phrases below. Then listen and check.**

The blue one | old red one | I was buying a new scooter | a new one

Mike What were you doing yesterday?
Tom 1.. .
Mike Which one?
Tom 2.. over there.
Mike It's cool!
Tom Yes, I really like it. Whose is that terrible 3... ?
Mike That's my scooter!
Tom I think you need to get 4..!

Skills

Listening

24 **1 Listen and number the story.**

Writing for your Portfolio

2 Write the story of Sandra and the boomerang. Use the beginnings of the sentences below and the pictures from Exercise 1.

1 Sandra was watching TV one night when ....
2 She ran upstairs and ....
3 The next day she took a printout of the photo ....
4 The next night, Sandra saw the object again. But this time ....
5 The day after, Sandra went into her classroom. ....
6 She put the object on the table ....
7 Suddenly ....
8 "Hey," Johnny said. ....

Skills

Reading

3 **Read the text and decide if the sentences are T (True) or F (False). Correct the false ones.**

TRUE LIFE STORIES

Robert McHammond was driving home one night with his wife, Jean, when their car suddenly stopped.
He turned the key but the car did not start. Jean looked at her watch. It was one minute before midnight and there were no other cars on the road. They were discussing what to do when they saw a bright light in the sky.

Robert opened the car door. Jean told him to stay in the car but he didn't listen. She watched her husband walk toward the light. He walked until he was under the light and stopped. Then suddenly the light disappeared and it was dark. It was also silent again. At the same time, the car started again. Jean looked at her watch again. It was still one minute to midnight. She waited for her husband but he didn't return. She called his name but there was no reply. Robert McHammond disappeared and his wife Jean never saw him again. ■

Dawn English was studying at her desk in her room for her final exam in history. But as time passed she began to feel a sharp pain in her arm.

She tried to call to her dad, but not a word came out. She got up and ran into the kitchen. "Dad, I'm in serious pain!"

Within minutes Dawn's dad had bandaged up her arm and put her in the car. He took her straight to the emergency room.

"I think it may be broken," said the doctor. "We may have to operate."

Suddenly Dawn's dad said "How's the studying going, Dawn? Do you want to have some dinner?"

"What?" said Dawn, confused. She then awoke on her pile of books with one very uncomfortable arm! ■

1 Robert and Jean were on a busy road. T / F ....

2 They saw a bright light in the night sky. T / F ....

3 Robert got out of the car. T / F ....

4 The whole encounter lasted for 20 minutes. T / F ....

5 Dawn went to bed because she was tired. T / F ....

6 In her dream she had a broken arm. T / F ....

7 The doctor told her to go home. T / F ....

8 Her father woke her up the next morning. T / F ....

UNIT 10 Shouldn't we ask?

1 Complete the dialogue using the phrases below.

we should ask | we're lost! | where's the theater | then turn left and it's there

Mike [1] ....
Sue Let's ask someone how to get there.
Mike I think [2] .... at the gas station.
Sue That's a good idea.
Mike Excuse me, [3] ....
Woman Cross the street and turn right on Fourth Street, [4] ...., right next to the supermarket.
Mike Thanks! Come on, Sue!

Using large numbers

2 Match the numbers with the amount in words.

A 6,223
B 624,332
C 632,434
D 63,323
E 63,232
F 6,232
G 64,232
H 632,324
I 6,323

1 ☐ six thousand, two hundred and thirty two.
2 ☐ sixty three thousand, two hundred and thirty two.
3 ☐ six hundred and thirty two thousand, three hundred and twenty four.
4 ☐ sixty three thousand, three hundred and twenty three.
5 ☐ six thousand, two hundred and twenty three.
6 ☐ sixty four thousand, two hundred and thirty two.
7 ☐ six hundred and twenty four thousand, three hundred and thirty two.
8 ☐ six thousand, three hundred and twenty three.
9 ☐ six hundred and thirty two thousand, four hundred and thirty four.

3 Write the prices in words.

forty seven million dollars.
....

....
....

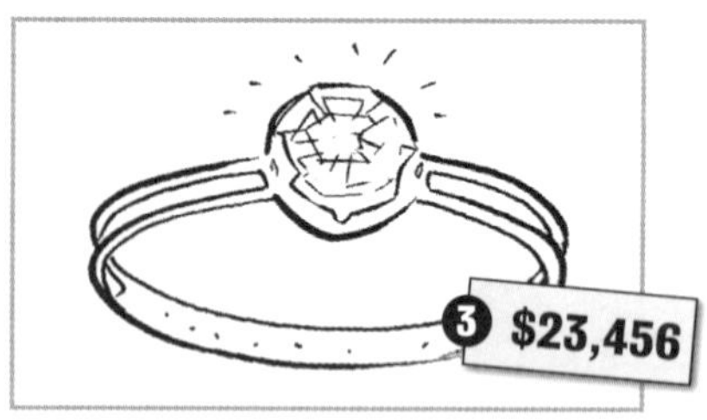

....
....

....
....

....
....

....
....

Language Focus

Vocabulary Directions and places

1 Where are these people going? Write sentences.

They're going to the mall. ....

She's ....

....

....

....

....

Talking about Asking for and giving directions

2 Read the dialogues and complete them with the words below.

cross ahead ~~straight~~ right second turn take far

1 **Tourist** Excuse me, where's the train station?
Salesclerk Go [1] straight ahead and take the [2] .... right.

2 **Tourist** Excuse me, where's the nearest bank?
Ticket clerk [3] .... the street and go as [4] .... as the theater.

3 **Man** Excuse me, where's the nearest post office?
Bank clerk [5] .... left, go to the theater and turn [6] ....

4 **Tourist** Excuse me, where's the Waldorf Hotel?
Post office clerk Go straight [7] .... Go past the cafe and [8] .... the first right.

Grammar

Should / shouldn't

1 Write each sentence under the correct picture.

~~You should go to bed.~~ You should say "sorry." You should see a doctor.
You shouldn't eat so much. You shouldn't drive so fast. You shouldn't go in there.

1 You should go to bed.

2 ....

3 ....

4 ....

5 ....

6 ....

2 Circle the correct verb form.

1 If you're tired, you *should / shouldn't* drive.
2 If you're going to live in Chile, you *should / shouldn't* learn some Spanish.
3 If your tooth hurts, you *should / shouldn't* see a dentist.
4 If you don't like horror movies, you *should / shouldn't* see *Blood Monsters*.
5 If you don't understand, you *should / shouldn't* ask your teacher.
6 If you like animals, you *should / shouldn't* visit the zoo. It's great.

3 Give advice for each sentence using the phrases below.

be a pilot read a good book take an aspirin get a job get a cat take a shower

1 Jill doesn't have any money
She should get a job.
2 I'm lonely.
....
3 Dave wants to travel the world.
....
4 Lenny is bored.
....
5 Paul has a headache.
....
6 I'm dirty from playing football.
....

4 Write advice.

1 John has a very important exam in the morning. He should go to bed early.
2 Ben and Tim are hungry. ....
3 Simon doesn't understand his science homework. ....
4 I'm angry with my younger sister. ....

Conjunctions *and / so / but / because*

5 Circle the correct word.

1 He's tired *because / so* he went to bed late last night.
2 Our grandparents live in Brazil, *but / so* we don't see them very often.
3 I really like going to the mall *but / and* hanging out with my friends.
4 I wanted to go to the party, *but / so* I wasn't invited.
5 I went to the show *but / because* my friend was in it.
6 I bought a new CD *and / so* left it in the store.

6 Complete the sentences with *and, so, but,* or *because*.

1 Paul did the dishes ....and..... broke a plate.

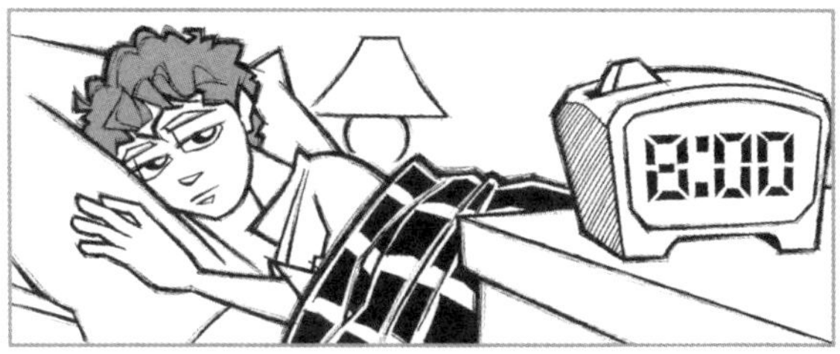

2 Tom went to bed early .... he was bored.

3 We went to the restaurant, ... it was closed.

4 They didn't like the movie, ... they left before the end.

5 We ordered pizza .... french fries.

6 Take a coat .... it's cold outside.

7 Complete the sentences about you.

1 I want to learn to drive because …

....

2 I want to learn to drive and …

....

3 I need more money so …

....

4 I need more money but …

....

5 I don't like science fiction movies but …

....

6 I don't like science fiction movies because …

....

7 I didn't go to school yesterday so …

....

8 I didn't go to school yesterday and …

....

Skills

Listening

25 **1** **Maria is explaining to the knight how to find the princess. Listen and follow the route. Write a D where the princess is.**

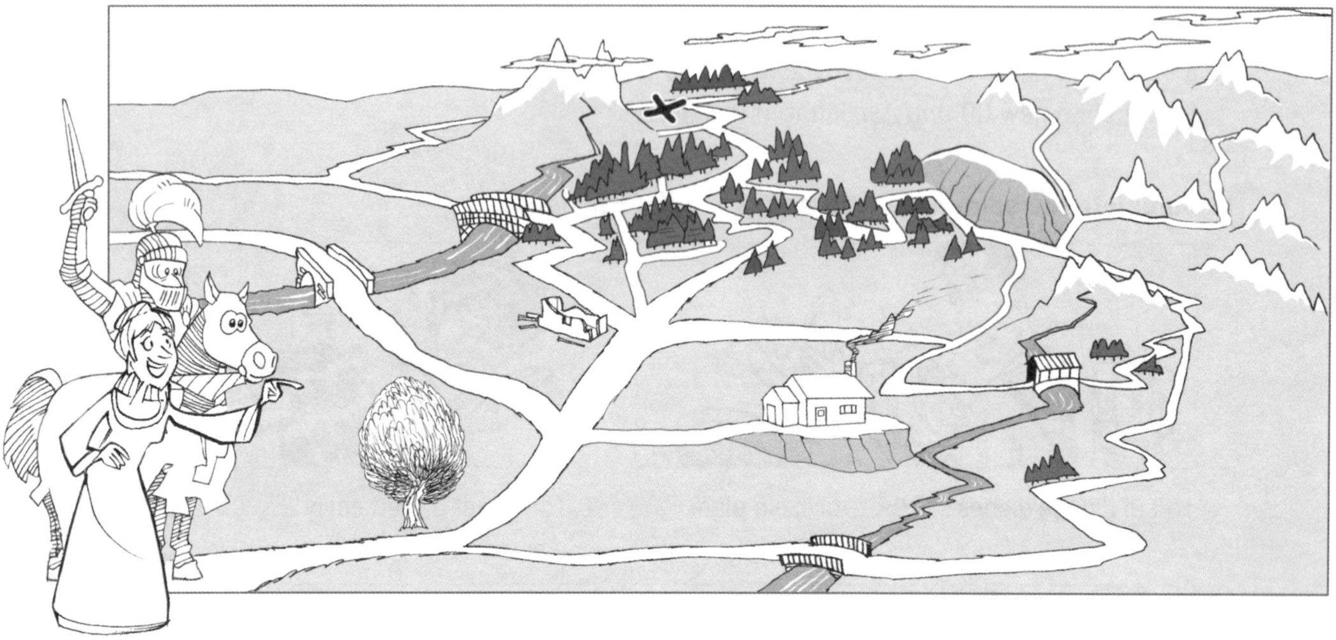

2 **The X on the map indicates where Maria lives. Find it and write a dialogue between the princess and the knight who wants to thank Maria for helping him.**

....
....
....
....
....
....

3 **Reorder the phrases to make a dialogue.**

☐	**Jasmin**	The Carlton? The movie is on at Maxwell Street. Hurry up!
☐	**Jasmin**	I'm also in front of the movie theater. The Maxwell Street Theater.
1	**Jasmin**	Hey, Ron, where are you?
☐	**Jasmin**	Go up Sixteenth Street and turn left after the bank.
☐	**Ron**	What's the quickest way to get there?
☐	**Ron**	I'm in front of the movie theater.
☐	**Ron**	OK. I'll be there in five minutes.
☐	**Ron**	Oh no! I must be at the wrong movie theater. I'm in front of the Carlton Theater.

Skills

Reading

4 **Read the text and answer the questions.**

The famous mathematician David Hilbert (1862–1943) was a genius, but often forgot simple things. He often forgot his keys or didn't remember where his glasses were. One day, the Hilberts moved to another house on another street. In the morning his wife gave him a piece of paper and said, "David, we're moving today, so I wrote the new address on this piece of paper." Hilbert's wife gave him the piece of paper, and he put it into his jacket pocket. At the university, he needed a piece of paper to make some notes. He remembered the piece of paper in his pocket. He took the paper out of his jacket. Then he wrote something on it and put it on the desk in his office. Some hours later, he left his office, but he didn't take the piece of paper with him.

Then he walked home. He went to the old address because he didn't remember what his wife said in the morning. But in front of the door he suddenly remembered. "Ah yes, a new house, a new address. Where's that piece of paper?" But of course he couldn't find it. It was on his desk at the university. Then he looked around and saw a girl. "Excuse me," he said. "Do you know where the Hilberts live now?" The girl answered, "Yes, Dad. Mom sent me to find you. I'll take you home now."

1 Who was David Hilbert?
2 When did he live?
3 What was on the piece of paper that his wife gave him?
4 Why did she give him this?
5 What did Professor Hilbert do with the paper first?
6 What did he do with the paper later?
7 When he walked home from the university, where did he go?
8 Who was the little girl?

Writing for your Portfolio

5 **Choose one of the two beginnings and write a story.**

☐ The party started at 9:00 p.m. I got off the train and walked out of the station. I put my hand in my pocket, but the piece of paper with the directions to Dave's house wasn't there...

☐ The sun was going down. It was getting dark. We were in the middle of a forest and we were lost...

UNIT 11 It won't rain

1 Complete the dialogue with the phrases below.

might rain | there's a breeze | That wouldn't be nice | would you like to come | why don't we

Mark 1 .... to the beach with us today?

Sue I don't know. I think it 2 ....

Mark Really? There aren't any clouds in the sky.

Sue Yes, but 3 .... and the weather forecast wasn't good.

Mark Well, I think it will be sunny all day.

Sue 4 .... go to the movies instead?

Mark Oh no! I don't want to be inside today. 5 .... Come on, Sue! Come to the beach!

Making excuses

2 Write the phrases under the correct picture.

No, we might break a window.
No, we might miss a touchdown.
No, it might fly away.
No, it might be poisonous.
No, I might break my leg.
No, that rock might fall on us.

....
....

....
....

....
....

....
....

....
....

....
....

Language Focus

Vocabulary Weather words

1 **Find and circle the weather words. Then write them under the correct picture.**

....

....

....

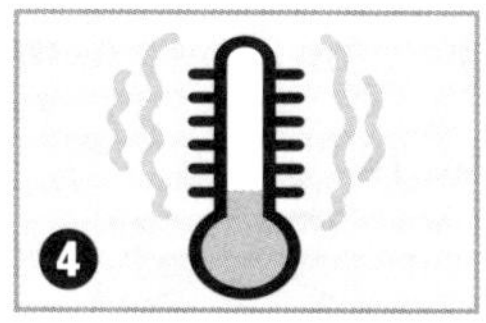

....

....

....

....

....

....

Talking about the weather

2 **Look at the map and write a weather report.**

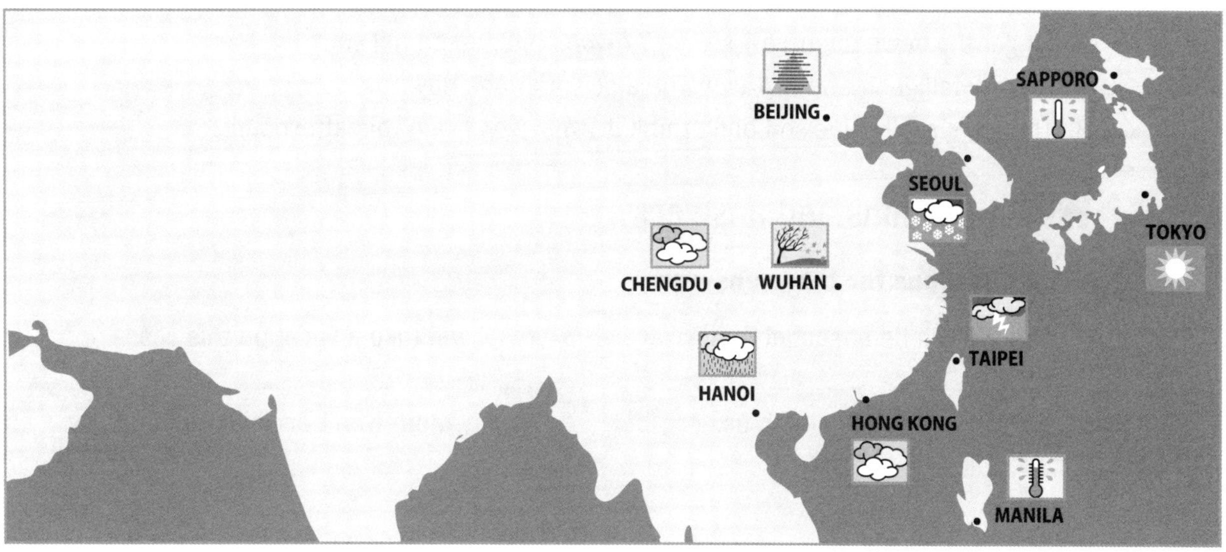

1 It will be sunny in Tokyo.
....

2 ....
....

3 ....
....

4 ....
....

5 ....
....

6 ....
....

7 ....
....

8 ....
....

Grammar

Will / won't

1 After each sentence, write "O" if it is an offer, "D" if it is a decision, or "P" if it is a prediction.

1 I'll help you carry your suitcase. O
2 It'll rain tomorrow. ....
3 I won't go to the movies tonight. ....
4 Brazil will win the next World Cup. ....
5 I think I'll go to Chile for vacation this year. ....
6 I'll pay for the meal. ....
7 The world will end in 1,000 years. ....
8 My mom can give you a ride home. ....

2 Rewrite the sentences using the short form.

1 I will see you tomorrow.
I'll see you tomorrow.
2 It will be sunny next week.
....
3 They will arrive on Sunday.
....
4 We will not be at school on Monday.
....
5 I will not tell anyone.
....
6 He will be famous one day.
....

3 Circle the correct word.

1 I'll leave early so I *will / won't* be late.
2 He's faster than me so I don't think I *will / won't* win the race.
3 It *will / won't* be cold, so take a warm coat.
4 It's a secret, so promise you *will / won't* tell anyone.
5 It's his first day at school so he *will / won't* know anybody.
6 I'll get the news tomorrow so I *will / won't* phone and tell you.
7 She's intelligent. She *will/won't* be a scientist one day.
8 The sky's really blue so I don't think it *will / won't* rain this afternoon.

Will Questions and answers

4 Write questions for these answers.

1 Yes, we will be at school tomorrow.
....
2 No, they won't come with us.
....
3 Yes, I will take a vacation this year.
....
4 No, my mom won't drive us to the party.
....

Sounds right 'll contraction

26

5 Listen and circle the sentences you hear.

1 a I'll see you tomorrow. b I'm seeing you tomorrow.
2 a It'll rain tomorrow. b It might rain tomorrow.
3 a They'll go to Mexico this year. b They go to Mexico this year.
4 a We'll do it. b We do it.
5 a You'll see him. b You see him.

Might / might not

6 Match the two halves of the sentence.

1 It might rain
2 I've got a headache
3 I need a new dress
4 I like Green Day
5 I drank a lot of soda today
6 I don't feel very hungry
7 I've seen this movie
8 He asked me to go to the prom

a and I might say "yes."
b so I might not eat anything.
c so I might not go to the party.
d so I might go shopping tomorrow.
e so take an umbrella.
f and I might not want to see it again.
g and I might buy their new album.
h so I might not sleep well tonight.

7 Reorder the words and write the complete sentences.

1 movies / I / to / the / might / go
I might go to the movies.

2 later / it / rain / might
....

3 date / go / might / on / we
....

4 want / not / go / might / she / to
....

5 be / late / might / they
....

6 think / to / might / I / bed / I / go
....

8 Complete with *might, will,* or *won't*.

1 I didn't sleep well last night, so I ....will.... be tired later.
2 The party starts at nine. I .... be late, I promise.
3 I .... help you make dinner. It'll be quicker with two.
4 He .... go to college, or he .... look for a job.
5 They .... win because they're not very good.
6 I .... go to the party on Friday. I'm not sure.

9 Write predictions about your future using *might / might not / will / won't*.

get married... > ....
.... < ...go to college
live in another country... > ....
.... < ...have children
earn a lot of money... > ....
.... < ...live in the country
be a rock star... > ....
.... < ...write a book

Skills

Listening

27 **1** **Look at the two maps of North America. Listen to the weather forecasts and draw the correct symbols.**

Key:

sunny: 

foggy: 

snowy: 

windy: 

rainy/showers: 

cloudy: 

stormy/ thunderstorms: 

28 **2** **Reorder the dialogues. Then listen and check.**

[1]	**Maria**	Hi, Robert, I'm taking the next train into the city. I'll be at your place at about six.
[ ]	**Maria**	I won't.
[ ]	**Maria**	What's the weather like there?
[ ]	**Robert**	Right now, it's fine. There might be some rain in the evening. Don't forget your umbrella.
[ ]	**Robert**	Great. I'll have dinner ready.

[1]	**Sue**	Where are you going?
[ ]	**Sue**	Why?
[ ]	**Sue**	You won't need it. We're getting a taxi.
[ ]	**Tom**	It looks like rain.
[ ]	**Tom**	Don't worry. I'll be back. I'm getting my raincoat.

Skills

Reading

3 **Read the story and decide if the sentences are T (True) or F (False).**

"And the weather for tomorrow…"

Dad Ok, let's finish packing! Don't forget your swimsuits!
Jane Dad, do I need to bring a sweater?
Dad No, I don't think so. It'll be sunny and warm in the south.
Newsreader …There will be heavy showers in the south tomorrow and Sunday, and temperatures will drop to 10° Celsius so it'll be a cold weekend. There might also be a few thunderstorms so…
Jamie Dad! Did you hear that? It's going to be cold! We can't go swimming!
Dad OK you'll have to bring along a sweater, too.
Jane And jackets and boots! It'll be wet and cold!
Jamie … and miserable!!!
Mom Don't worry, we'll still have a nice time. Just pack some extra clothes.

(15 minutes later)

Dad OK, we're finished! Do we have everything? Jamie, turn off the TV!
Jamie Look, the weather's on again.
Mom Let's hear what it says.
Newsreader I'm very sorry, but I gave you last week's weather report. Now, here's the correct weather report for the weekend. The south will be sunny with high temperatures of 25° to 30° Celsius. It will be cloudy in the evenings, but there won't be any rain and definitely no thunderstorms. My apologies again for giving you the wrong information…
Jamie Great news! It'll be sunny!

1 Their bags are packed when they hear the first weather forecast. T / F
2 The first weather forecast says it will be wet and cold on the weekend. T / F
3 They want to go swimming. T / F
4 When they finish packing, Jamie turns off the TV. T / F
5 The newsreader gave them the correct forecast the first time. T / F
6 The newsreader says that there will be some thunderstorms over the weekend. T / F

Writing for your Portfolio

4 **You are on vacation with your family. Write a postcard to a friend saying:**

- where you are and what you are doing
- where you are going tomorrow
- what the weather is like

UNIT 12 What if...?

1 Complete the dialogue using the words below.

on beach won't don't will too

Tom Where are we going [1]............................ vacation this year?

Sally I want to go to Paris. It's so amazing!

Dad And expensive! If we go there we [2]..................... have any money to spend. It's too expensive. What about going to the Rocky Mountains?

Tom I don't want to go there. I want to go to a [3]..................... .

Mom Well, why [4]............................ we stay at home? It's cheap and there are a lot of places to go.

Sally But if we stay here we [5]......................... never see the sun. It always rains!

Dad What about going to the lake? It's not [6]................... expensive and the weather is good. We can drive there, too!

Sally/Tom Oh no, Dad! Not another road trip!

Talking about alternatives

2 Complete the dialogue with a question and its answer.

Bs But what if the ocean's too rough?
But what if it's too expensive?
But what if there are none in the store?

As I'll get that Jackie Chan movie.
We'll just lie on the beach.
We'll go to the burger place.

1 **A** Let's get Tom the new Keane CD for his birthday.
B *But what if he already has it?*
A *He can exchange it for something else.*

2 **A** I want to buy the new James Bond DVD.
B ....
A ....

3 **A** We're going to have lunch at the pizza place.
B ....
A ....

4 **A** Let's go surfing.
B ....
A ....

Language Focus

Vocabulary Vacations

1 What do these people want to do on vacation? Write sentences.

1 Henry wants to lie on the beach.

2 Dana wants to ....

3 Robin wants to ....

4 Jan wants to ....

5 Byron wants to ....

6 Jasmine wants to ....

Suggestions and preferences

2 Complete the mini-dialogues with the sentences below.

I'd rather stay in a hotel. I'd rather go to the beach. I'd rather send him a postcard.

1 **A** Let's stay with relatives. **B** ....

2 **A** Let's go sightseeing. **B** ....

3 **A** Let's buy Jim a souvenir. **B** ....

3 Write similar dialogues. Use the prompts.

1 camping / hiking **A** ....
B ....

2 sightseeing / souvenirs **A** ....
B ....

3 Thailand / Singapore **A** ....
B ....

4 with relatives / friends **A** ....
B ....

Grammar

If clauses

1 Match the phrases to form a sentence in the first conditional.

1 If you wear that shirt,
2 If you invite her to the theater,
3 If you touch that dog,
4 If it's hot tomorrow,
5 If I call you at nine,
6 If he drives that fast,
7 If we leave now,
8 If I give you some money,

a it'll bite you.
b will you be home?
c he'll have an accident.
d we'll be home by 10.
e you'll look really good.
f will you buy a sandwich for me?
g we'll go to the beach.
h I'm sure she'll say "yes."

2 Circle the correct word.

1 If we *miss / will miss* the bus, we *take / will take* a taxi.
2 If you *don't eat / won't eat* fruit, you *get / will get* a cold.
3 If you *help / will help* me, I *lend / will lend* you that *Beyoncé* CD.
4 If he *doesn't stop / won't stop* eating so much, he *has / will have* problems later.
5 You *are / will be* on time if you *run / will run.*
6 She *goes / will go* to the party if you *invite / will invite* her.
7 They *see / will see* the new Lara Croft movie if they *go / will go* to the theater.
8 I *come / will come* over to your house if you *rent / will rent* a DVD.

3 Write questions using the words below.

1 What / you do / rain / on the weekend?
What will you do if it rains on the weekend?
2 What show / you watch / turn on the TV tonight?
....
3 What / you eat / feel hungry / after dinner tonight?
....
4 Where / you go / go away / this weekend?
....
5 What / you play / play a sport / this weekend?
....
6 Who / you talk to / call someone / tonight?
....

4 Write answers for the questions above.

1 If it rains this weekend, I'll stay home and study for my test on Monday.
2 ....
3 ....
4 ....
5 ....
6 ....

Possessive pronouns

5 **Complete the table.**

Possessive adjective	Possessive pronoun
my	1 mine
your	2 ....
his	3 ....
her	4 ....
our	5 ....
your	6 ....
their	7 ....

6 **Circle the correct adjective or possessive pronoun.**

1 Don't touch it. It's *my / mine.*
2 Is this *your / yours*? I'm sorry, I didn't know.
3 Is that *her / hers* new car?
4 See that dog? It's *our / ours.*
5 Are these *your / yours* children?
6 I'm not sure but I think it's *their / theirs.*
7 I'll write down *our / ours* address for you.

Questions with *Whose...?*

7 **Write questions about the pictures below.**

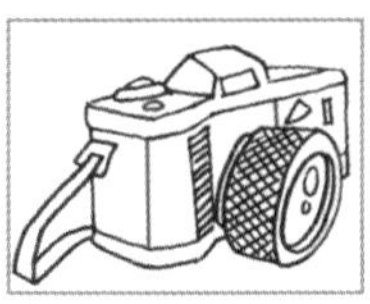
1 Whose camera is this?

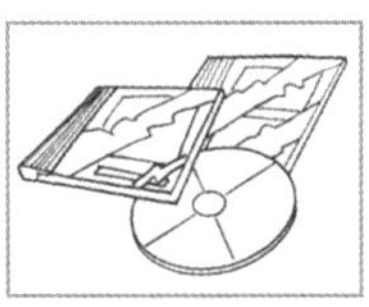
2 ....

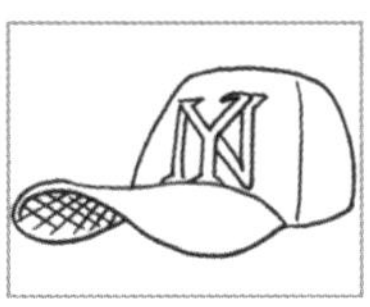
3 ....

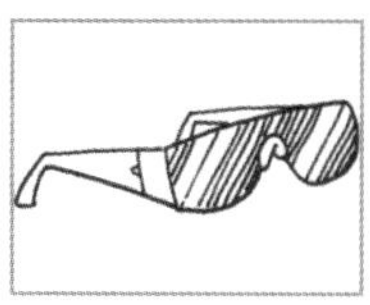
4 ....

5 ....

6 ....

8 **Write answers using possessive pronouns.**

1 It's Jane's camera. It's hers.
2 They're Kevin and my CDs. ....
3 It's my baseball cap. ....
4 They're Dad's sunglasses. ....
5 They're Helen's sneakers. ....
6 It's Dave and Sue's house. ....

Grammar for Communication

29 **Complete the dialogue using the phrases below. Then listen and check.**

in the school gym | on the weekend | they say no | what if

Martin Let's have a party [1]... before summer vacation.
Susan OK. Where?
Martin Let's ask the school if we can have it [2]... .
Susan But [3]... the school is closed?
Martin Well then we can ask the pizza place.
Susan But what if [4]... .
Martin Then I'll ask my parents—and don't say "But what if …"

Skills

Reading

1 **Read the dairy of Jeremy White. On which day does he do these things?**

1 Jeremy has an argument with his dad. ....
2 Jeremy runs a race. ....
3 Jeremy makes a list. ....
4 Jeremy is late for school. ....
5 Jeremy gets his exam results. ....

SUNDAY

Fantastic. Great. Wonderful. Finally, it's here! The last week of school for three whole months. Three months of vacation! Oh, what a happy week!

"Things to do for my vacation"
- Paint my bedroom blue.
- Take karate lessons.
- Beat my dad at chess.
- Read all the "Lemony Snicket" books, again!
- Get in shape!
- Build a new go-kart with Sam.

MONDAY

School was a bit boring. I got my report card. I got "C" for everything, but "C" isn't so bad. It's better than "D." I explained this to Dad. He didn't really understand. I don't think he's very happy at the moment. I think he has problems at work.

Four days to go!

My go-kart

TUESDAY

I had a big argument with my dad at breakfast today. He says I can't paint my bedroom blue. It has to be white. White! My dad doesn't understand teenagers. I'm not going to speak to him for a week. School was better. We played games all day. I think our teachers are very tired.

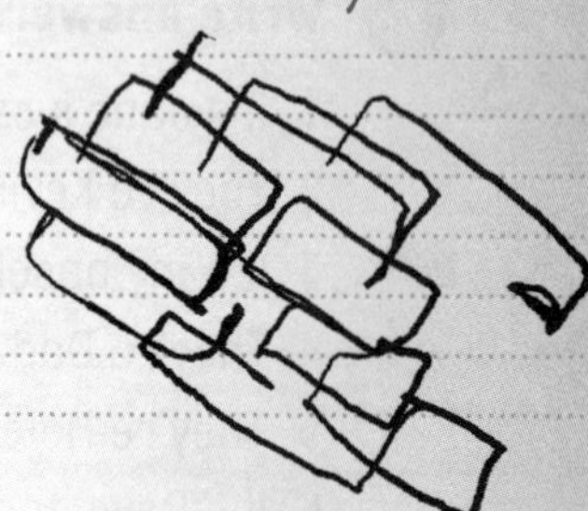

Skills

Listening

30 **2** **Listen to what Jeremy wrote in his journal on Friday. Circle the correct answer.**

1 His principal's name is:
   a Mr. Hill.
   b Mrs. White.
   c Miss Hall.

2 At the school assembly the principal read out the names of:
   a the students who are leaving.
   b the teachers who are leaving.
   c the best students.

3 The principal said Jeremy's name because:
   a he was one of the best students.
   b he was talking.
   c he was sleeping.

4 Jeremy's new plan is to:
   a call Jenny the next day.
   b talk to her when he's 14.
   c send her an email.

Writing for your Portfolio

3 **Write a page for a dairy about your last day of school.**

....

....

....

....

....

....

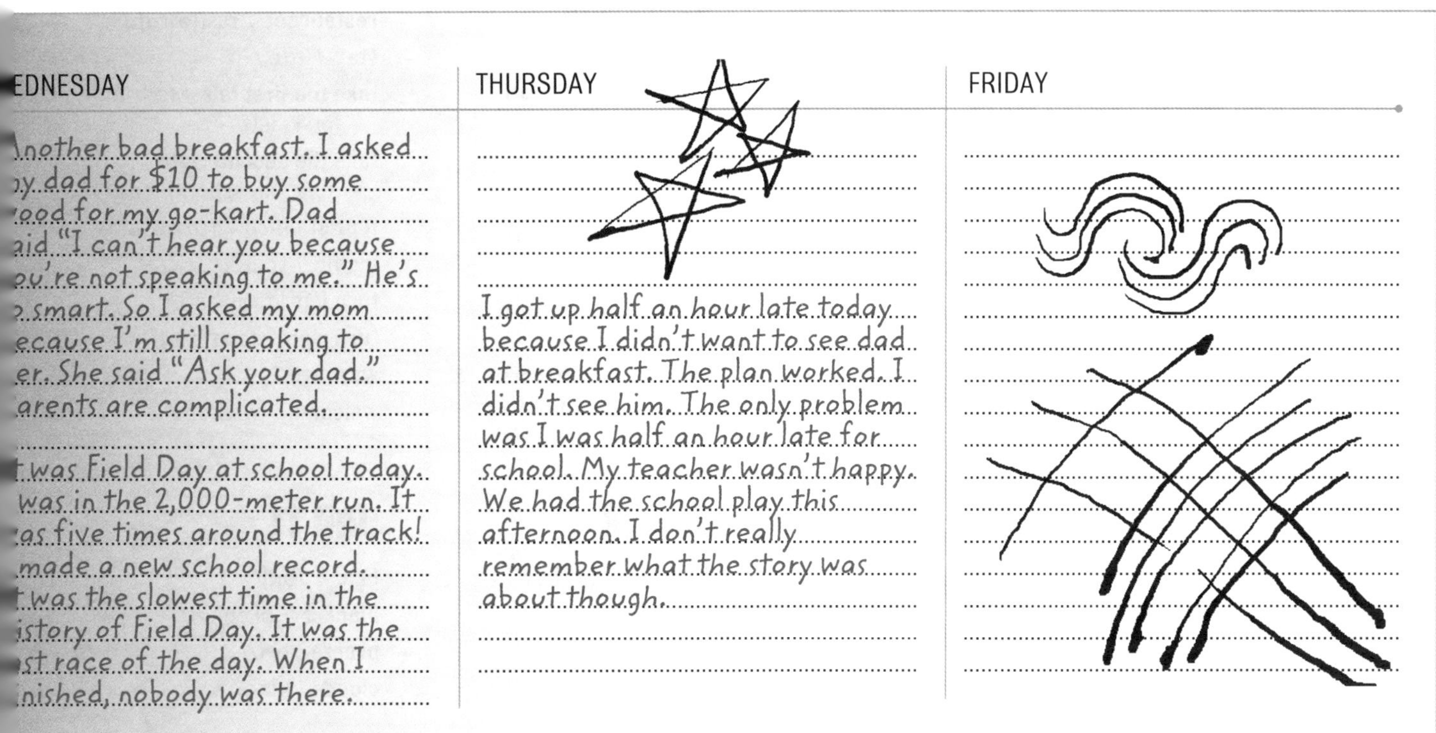
EDNESDAY

nother bad breakfast. I asked
y dad for $10 to buy some
ood for my go-kart. Dad
aid "I can't hear you because
ou're not speaking to me." He's
smart. So I asked my mom
ecause I'm still speaking to
er. She said "Ask your dad."
arents are complicated.

t was Field Day at school today.
was in the 2,000-meter run. It
as five times around the track!
made a new school record.
t was the slowest time in the
istory of Field Day. It was the
st race of the day. When I
nished, nobody was there.

THURSDAY

I got up half an hour late today because I didn't want to see dad at breakfast. The plan worked. I didn't see him. The only problem was I was half an hour late for school. My teacher wasn't happy. We had the school play this afternoon. I don't really remember what the story was about though.

FRIDAY

Wordlist

Unit 7

basketball /'bɑskɪtbəl/
to come back /kʌm 'bæk/
bike riding /'baɪk ridɪŋ/
dinner /'dɪnər/
fan /fæn/
to get up late /ˌgɛt ʌp 'leɪt/
to go fishing /goʊ 'fɪʃɪŋ/
to go shopping /goʊ 'ʃɑpɪŋ/
to go to a friend's house /ˌgoʊ tu ə 'frɛndz ˌhaʊs/
to go to the movies /ˌgoʊ tə ðə 'moʊviz/
to hang out /hæŋ 'aʊt/
interested /'ɪnt(ə)rəstəd/
to listen to music /ˌlɪsən tə 'myuzɪk/
mountain biking /'maʊntən ˌbaɪkɪŋ/
mountain climbing /'maʊntən ˌklaɪmɪŋ/
packed lunch /pækt 'lʌntʃ/
paper route /'peɪpə raʊnd/
plan /plæn/

to play sports /pleɪ 'spɔrts/
to remember /rɪ'mɛmbər/
running /'rʌnɪŋ/
to sell /sɛl/
skateboarding /'skeɪtbɔrdɪŋ/
skating /'skeɪtɪŋ/
surfing /'sʌrfɪŋ/
swimming /'swɪmɪŋ/
theme park /'θim pɑrk/
trampolining /træmpə'linɪŋ/
to watch sports /wɑtʃ 'spɔrts/

Unit 8

anaconda /ˌænə'kɑndə/
ankle /'æŋkəl/
antelope /'æntəˌloʊp/
aspirin /'æsp(ə)rən/
attack /ə'tæk/
backache /'bækˌeɪk/
blue whale /blu 'hweɪl/
a cold /ə 'koʊld/
dentist /'dɛntɪst/
dolphin /'dɑlfən/
earache /'ɪreɪk/
environment /ɪn'vaɪrə(n)mənt/
giraffe /ʤə'rɑf/
a glass of water /ə ˌglæs əv wɔtər/
head /hɛd/
headache /'hɛdˌeɪk/
to hurt /hərt/
knee /ni/
lemonade /lɛmə'neɪd/
lion /'laɪən/
lucky /'lʌki/
medicinal /mə'dɪsnəl/
ostrich /'ɑstrɪtʃ/
oxygen /'ɑksɪʤən/
painting /'peɪntɪŋ/
pig /pɪg/
plant /plænt/
project /'prɑʤɛkt/
rain forest /'reɪn fɔrəst/
rhinoceros /raɪ'nɑsərəs/
romantic /roʊ'mæntɪk/
safe /seɪf/
sick /sɪk/
sore throat /sɔr 'θroʊt/
stomach /'stʌmək/
stomachache /'stəmək ˌeɪk/
streetlight /'strit leɪt/
toe /toʊ/
toothache /'tuθˌeɪk/
to wake /weɪk/
whale shark /'hweɪl ʃɑrk/

Unit 9

air /ɛr/
aliens /'eɪliənz/
around /əraʊnd/
to block /blɑk/
bored /bɔrd/
button /'bʌtən/
to carry /'kæri/
coffee /'kɑfi/
comfortable /'kʌm(p)(f)tərbəl/
country /'kʌntri/
to cry /kraɪ/
to destroy /dɪ'strɔɪ/
dirty /'dərti/
frightened /'fraɪtənd/
garbage can /gɑrbɪʤ kæn/
gas company /'gæs ˌkʌmpəni/
gas leak /'gæs lik/
to go out /goʊ 'aʊt/
huge /hyuʤ/
key /ki/
to land /lænd/
lights /laɪts/
to lock /lɑk/
loud /laʊd/
mask /mæsk/
palace /'pæləs/
path /pæθ/
to pick up /pɪk 'ʌp/
place /pleɪs/
planet /'plænət/
to push /pʊʃ/
to run away /rʌn ə'weɪ/
salt /sɔlt/
seed /sid/
shocked /ʃɑkt/
silver /'sɪlvər/
spaceship /'speɪsʃɪp/
to steal /stil/
still /stɪl/
suddenly /'sʌdənli/
surprised /sə(r)'praɪzd/
thrilled /θrɪld/
to turn around /tərn ə'raʊnd/
universe /'yunəvərs/
world /wər(ə)ld/

Unit 10

to be lost /bi 'lɔst/
to cross /krɔs/
crowd /kraʊd/
directions /də'rɛkʃənz/
to explain /ɪk'spleɪn/
to fall asleep /fɔl ə'slip/
to figure something out /fɪgyər...'aʊt/
gas station /gæs steɪʃən/
go as far as the… /'goʊ əz ˌfɑr əz ðə/
go past the… /'goʊ pæst ðə/
to go around in circles /ˌgoʊ əraʊnd ɪn 'sərkəlz/
go straight ahead /ˌgoʊ streɪt ə'hɛd/
hospital /'hɑspɪtəl/
hotel /hoʊ'tɛl/
map /mæp/
now /naʊ/
one hundred /ˌwʌn 'hʌndrəd/
one hundred thousand /wʌn ˌhʌndrəd 'θaʊzənd/
one million /wʌnˌ mɪ(l)yən/
one thousand /ˌwʌn 'θaʊzənd/
police station /pə'lis ˌsteɪʃən/
post office /'poʊst ˌɑfəs/
to rent a DVD /ˌrɛnt ə ˌdi vi 'di/
restaurant /'rɛst(ə)rɑnt/
star /stɑr/
take the first left /ˌteɪk ðə ˌfərst 'lɛft/
take the second right /ˌteɪk ðə ˌsɛkənd 'raɪt/
tourist office /'tʊrɪst ˌɑfəs/
traffic /'træfɪk/
turn left /tərn 'lɛft/
turn right /tərn 'raɪt/
way /weɪ/
welcome /'wɛlkəm/

Unit 11

beach /bitʃ/
blanket /'blæŋkət/
breeze /briz/
clouds /klaʊdz/

cloudy /ˈklaʊdi/

to come out /kʌm ˈaʊt/

championship /ˈʧæmpiənʃɪp/

college /kɑlɪʤ/

degree /dɪˈgri/

explorer /ɪkˈsplɔrər/

famous /ˈfeɪməs/

fog /fɔg/

foggy /ˈfɔgi/

to get married /ˌgɛt ˈmɛrid/

no way /noʊ ˈweɪ/

outside /aʊtˈsaɪd/

to pass /pæs/

race /reɪs/

rain /reɪn/

rainy /ˈreɪni/

rich /rɪʧ/

showers /ˈʃaʊ(ə)rz/

sky /skaɪ/

snow /snoʊ/

snowy /ˈsnoʊi/

sun /sʌn/

sunny /ˈsʌni/

thunderstorm /ˈθʌndərstɔrm/

upstairs /ˌʌpˈstɛrz/

windy /ˈwɪndi/

Unit 12

to agree /əˈgri/

bell /bɛl/

to book /bʊk/

discount /ˈdɪskaʊnt/

to discuss /dɪˈskʌs/

down /daʊn/

to freeze /friz/

to go on vacation /goʊ ɔn veɪˈkeɪʃən/

to go sightseeing /goʊ ˈsaɪtsiɪŋ/

idea /aɪˈdiə/

magazine /ˈmægəˌzin/

to organize /ˈɔrgənaɪz/

postcard /ˈpoʊs(t)kɑrd/

relatives /ˈrɛlətɪvz/

sunscreen /ˈsʌnkrin/

trouble /ˈtrʌbəl/

would rather /wʊd ˈræðər/

weather /ˈwɛðər/

Pronunciation guide

Vowels

/i/	**rea**l, scr**ee**n
/ɪ/	d**i**sh, s**i**t
/ɛ/	ch**e**ss, b**e**d
/æ/	b**a**d, t**a**xi
/ʌ/	m**u**st, d**o**ne
/ʊ/	g**oo**d, f**u**ll
/u/	ch**oo**se, vi**ew**
/ə/	dr**a**matic, th**e**
/ɑ/	st**o**p, **o**pera
/ɔ/	s**aw**, d**au**ghter

Vowels + /r/

/ər/	f**ir**st, sh**ir**t
/ɑr/	c**ar**
/ɔr/	h**or**se
/ɛr/	th**eir**
/ʊr/	t**our**ist
/ɪr/	**ear**

Diphthongs

/eɪ/	pl**ay**, tr**ai**n
/aɪ/	**i**ce, n**igh**t
/ɔɪ/	empl**oy**er, n**oi**sy
/aʊ/	h**ou**se, d**ow**nload
/oʊ/	n**o**, wind**ow**

Consonants

/p/	**p**ush
/b/	**b**ank
/t/	**t**ime
/d/	**d**iary
/k/	**c**arpet
/g/	bi**g**
/f/	sur**f**
/v/	**v**ery
/θ/	**th**in
/ð/	**th**at
/s/	**s**it
/z/	**z**ero
/ʃ/	**sh**ine
/ʒ/	mea**s**ure
/h/	**h**ot
/w/	**w**ater
/ʧ/	**ch**air
/ʤ/	**j**oke
/m/	**m**ore
/n/	s**n**ow
/ŋ/	si**ng**
/r/	**r**ing
/l/	sma**ll**
/y/	**y**ou

Grammar Review

Present continuous for future — Unit 7

The *present continuous* is used for a planned future action.
He's meeting *the president on Monday.*

I'm talking *to him tomorrow.*
They are seeing *her on Tuesday.*
Are you going *tomorrow?*
We aren't playing *football tomorrow.*

Superlatives — Unit 8

The superlative
The superlative form of one-syllable adjectives and two-syllable adjectives ending in **-e**, **-er**, **-ow**, **-y** follows the pattern:
the + **adjective** + **-est**
She is ***the*** *tall****est*** *in her class.*

The superlative has the same spelling rules as the comparative.

The superlative of all the other adjectives is formed by putting **the most** before the positive.
It's ***the most*** *interesting book I've ever read.*

Superlatives are often followed by **of** or **in**.

She is the most intelligent **of** *them all.*
She is the smallest ***in*** *the class.*

Adjectives which have irregular comparative forms also have irregular superlatives:
good = **the best** / bad = **the worst** / far = **the farthest**

Past continuous — Unit 8

The *past continuous* tense has the following structure:
Subject + **simple past** of **be** + **-ing** form of the main verb

Positive	**Negative**	**Questions**	**Short answers**
I was playing	I wasn't playing	Was I playing?	Yes, I was. / No, I wasn't.
you were playing	you weren't playing	Were you playing?	Yes, you were. / No, you weren't.
he was playing	he wasn't playing	Was he playing?	Yes, he was. / No, he wasn't.
she was playing	she wasn't playing	Was she playing?	Yes, she was. / No, she wasn't.
it was playing	it wasn't playing	Was it playing?	Yes, it was. / No, it wasn't.
we were playing	we weren't playing	Were we playing?	Yes, we were. / No, we weren't.
you were playing	you weren't playing	Were you playing?	Yes, you were. / No, you weren't.
they were playing	they weren't playing	Were they playing?	Yes, they were. / No, they weren't

The *past continuous* is used to express a continuous action in the past:
*What **were you doing** at eight o'clock this morning?*
***I was watching** the* Morning Show *on TV.*

Past continuous vs. simple past — Unit 9

The *past continuous* expresses an action that continued for some time in the past. The *simple past* is used for actions completed in the past. To express an action happening at a certain time while another action was already happening, we use the *past continuous + simple past*:
***We were having** dinner when the telephone **rang**.*

One / ones — Unit 9

To avoid repetition, a noun that has already appeared can be replaced by **one** for the singular and by **ones** for the plural:
*Which book is yours? The blue **one** or the red **one**?*
*I don't like watching old movies, I prefer modern **ones**.*

A lot of / much / many — Unit 9

A lot of can be used with countable and uncountable nouns, in affirmative, interrogative, and negative sentences. However, it is better to use **a lot of** in affirmative sentences, **much** (with noncount or singular nouns) and **many** (with count or plural nouns) in negative and interrogative sentences:
*We have **a lot of** friends.*
*Did you see **many** people?*
*I haven't seen **many** people today.*
*She didn't spend **much** money.*

Should for advice — Unit 10

Should has the same form for all persons and can be used for advice.
The negative form of **should** is **shouldn't**.
*You **should** take an umbrella, it's raining.*
*She **shouldn't** work so late.*

Conjunctions *and / so / but / because* — Unit 10

We use **and** to join ideas and add information.
*Cross the street **and** turn left.*

We use **so** to talk about a solution or conclusion.
*We're tired, **so** let's go home.*

We use **but** to talk about an opposing event / point of view.
*He left early, **but** he was still late.*

We use **because** to give a reason.
*He was tired **because** he stayed out late.*

Might / might not

Unit 11

Might (**might not**) has the same form for all persons. It is a conditional and expresses possibility in the future.
*It **might** rain or it **might not**, I don't know.*

Will

Unit 11

Will is used to express expectation, hope, or prediction of a future event. The conjugation follows the pattern: **Subject** + **will** (**'ll**) + **infinitive** without "to" of the main verb.
*I think she **will** (she' **ll**) **come** with us.*

Will can also be used to express an immediate decision, a promise, or an offer. In this case, it is usually contracted to '**ll**:
*I'**ll** do it.*
*I'**ll help you**.*

will + **not** (contraction **won't**) is used in the negative form.
*She **won't** be here next week.*

In the interrogative form, **will** comes before the subject:
*When **will** he come back?*

Conditional type 1

Unit 12

The *first conditional* (or *type one*) sentence expresses what will probably happen if a certain situation comes true. It consists of an **if-clause** expressing a condition and a **main clause** expressing the consequence determined by the **if-clause**:
***If it rains**, **I will stay** home.*

The verb in the **if-clause** is in the *simple present,* while the verb in the **main clause** is in the future with **will**.
The meaning does not change if the **main clause** comes before the **if-clause**:
***I will stay** at home **if** it **rains**.*
In this case we don't put a comma between the **main clause** and the **if-clause**.

Both the **if-clause** and the **main clause** can be positive or negative:
*If it **doesn't** rain, I **won't** stay at home.*
It is possible to have a conditional sentence with the interrogative form of the **main clause**:
***Will** you stay at home if it **rains**?*

Short answers follow the general rule:
Yes, I will / No, I won't.

Possessive pronouns

Unit 12

The possessive pronouns are:

Singular	Plural
mine	ours
yours	yours
his hers	theirs

Possessive pronouns have the same characteristics as possessive adjectives and are invariable. In the third person singular, they refer to the possessor.

*Whose book is that? It's **Marco's**. It's **his.***
*Whose bag is that? It's **Maria's**. It's **hers.***

Whose ...?

Unit 12

Possessive pronouns are often used to answer a question introduced by the interrogative adjective or pronoun *whose*?
Whose** book is this? It's **mine**, **yours, etc.

Instruções de uso do CD-ROM

Instalação

Insira o CD-ROM **American MORE!** no compartimento de CD e siga na tela as instruções de instalação.
Se as instruções não aparecerem na tela, entre em *Meu Computador*, clique em D (ou no *drive* apropriado). Em seguida dê um duplo-clique no ícone *American More!* para iniciar a instalação.
Para usar o CD-ROM, dê um duplo-clique no atalho **American MORE!** criado na área de trabalho.

Conteúdo do CD-ROM

Exercícios interativos complementares para prática de vocabulário, gramática, pronúncia, leitura, compreensão oral e produção escrita, além de jogos divertidos. Clique em uma das unidades (Starter-12) e selecione uma das atividades para começar.

Configurações de sistema recomendadas

Windows 2000/XP/: 256MB RAM (mín. 512 MB)
Windows Vista/7: 1GB RAM (mín. 2GB)

Suporte

Para resolver problemas técnicos relacionados ao uso deste CD-ROM, acesse: www.cambridge.org/elt/multimedia/help

Workbook 2 – Audio CD

Track	Time	Track	Time	Track	Time	Track	Time
1.	0'52"	9.	1'08"	17.	1'09"	25.	1'31"
2.	1'09"	10.	0'52"	18.	0'48"	26.	0'41"
3.	1'05"	11.	1'29"	19.	0'55"	27.	0'59"
4.	1'20"	12.	0'56"	20.	1'35"	28.	0'57"
5.	1'18"	13.	1'39"	21.	0'47"	29.	0'45"
6.	1'45"	14.	0'47"	22.	3'19"	30.	0'58"
7.	0'37"	15.	0'51"	23.	0'41"		
8.	0'47"	16.	1'00"	24.	1'56"		

Total Duration: 34min36s